D1541470

Be Patient–
I'm Not Perfect Yet

The Fruit of the Spirit

J U A N I T A   P U R C E L L

BAPTIST CHURCH

REGULAR BAPTIST PRESS
1300 North Meacham Road
Schaumburg, Illinois 60173-4806

Quotations on pages 11, 13, and 34 are from *The Bible Exposition Commentary*, vol. 1, by Warren W. Wiersbe. © 1989 by SP Publications, Inc., Wheaton, IL 60187. Published by Victor Books. Used by permission.

Quotation on page 19 is from *The Elisabeth Elliot Newsletter,* July/August 1991. Used by permission.

Quotations on pages 22 and 61 are from *My Utmost for His Highest* by Oswald Chambers. © 1935 by Dodd, Mead & Company, Inc. Used by permission of Emily Coth.

Quotations on pages 23, 31, and 32 are from *A Lamp for My Feet* by Elisabeth Elliot. © 1985; Servant Publications, Ann Arbor, MI. Used by permission.

Quotations on pages 25 and 43 are from *I Love the Word Impossible* by Ann Kiemel. © 1976 by Tyndale House Publishers, Wheaton, IL. Used by permission.

Quotations on pages 35, 44, and 45 are from *How to Say No to a Stubborn Habit* by Erwin W. Lutzer. © 1979 by SP Publications, Inc., Wheaton, IL 60187. Published by Victor Books. Used by permission.

Quotations on pages 39–44 are from *Self-Confrontation: An In-Depth Discipleship Manual* by John Broger. © 1978, revised 1991; Biblical Counseling Foundation, Rancho Mirage, CA. Used by permission.

Quotations on page 42, 57, 70, and 89 are from *The Fruit of the Spirit* by Leroy Brownlow. © 1982, 1989 by Leroy Brownlow. Brownlow Publishing Company, Fort Worth, TX. Used by permission.

Quotation on page 50 is from *Seeking God* by Joni Earickson Tada. © 1991; Word, Inc., Dallas, TX. Used by permission.

Quotation on pages 55 and 56 is from *The Applause of Heaven* by Max Lucado. © 1990; Word, Inc., Dallas, TX. Used by permission.

Quotation on page 63 is from *From the Father's Heart* by Charles Slagle. © 1989 by Charles Slagle. Used by permission of Destiny Image Publishers. All rights reserved.

Quotations on pages 67, 68, 75, and 76 are from *The Practice of Godliness* by Jerry Bridges. © 1983; NavPress, Colorado Springs, CO. Used by permission.

Quotation on page 68 is from *A Gardener Looks at the Fruits of the Spirit* by Phillip Keller. © 1979; Word, Inc., Dallas, TX. Used by permission.

Quotation on page 71, "Show a Little Bit of Love and Kindess," is © coypright 1974 by John W. Peterson Music Company. All rights reserved. Used by permission.

Quotation on page 74 is from *Light from Many Lamps*, edited by Lillian Eichler Watson. © 1951. Used by permission.

Quotations on pages 82 and 95 are from *Discipline: The Glad Surrender* by Elisabeth Elliot. Used by permission of Baker Book House. © 1982 by Elisabeth Elliot Gren.

Quotation on page 83 is from *Is My Head on Straight?* by Phyllis C. Michael. © 1976 by Word, Inc., Dallas, TX. Used by permission of Phyllis C. Michael, owner.

Quotations on pages 84, 85, and 99 are taken from *The Power of Commitment* by Jerry White. © 1985; NavPress, Colorado Springs, CO. Used by permission.

Quotation on page 97 is from *30 Days to Understanding the Christian Life* by Max Anders. © 1990; Word, Inc., Dallas, Texas. Used by permission.

Quotation on pages 98 and 99 is from *Closer Walk,* June 1991; copyright 1991; Walk Thru the Bible Ministries, Atlanta, GA. Used by permission.

BE PATIENT—I'M NOT PERFECT YET
© 1993
Regular Baptist Press
Schaumburg, Illinois
1-800-727-4440 • www.regularbaptistpress.org
RBP5214 • ISBN: 0-87227-178-1

Printed in U.S.A.

Seventh printing—2003

CONTENTS

A Special Thanks

To Valerie Wilson, editor of RBP Women's Studies, who believed in me and my writing enough to help me get started. Whenever I've needed advice or help, she has always been there for me and is a continuing source of encouragement.

PREFACE

Do you ever feel as if you are taking two steps forward and three steps backward in your walk with Christ? You just get one sin conquered, and now you have to battle another one? Don't get discouraged! I feel the same way! Struggling with the flesh is a daily battle. But, praise God, we're still struggling! We may be hobblin' and wobblin', but at least we're still walking.

Yes, be thankful you are still fighting the enemy of your soul, Satan. He has one goal for your life: defeat. He will keep whispering in your ear, "Give up; it isn't worth the struggle"; or, "If God really loved you, He wouldn't make life so tough for you." Many Christian women have listened to Satan and have fallen by the wayside. The enemy now controls their lives, and they are fulfilling the lusts of the flesh listed in Galatians 5:19–21. Their lives are filled with anger, hatred, bitterness, greed, jealousy, adultery—and the list goes on. What a terrible exchange these people have made! If they had just kept climbing, they could have learned to walk in the Spirit. Flowing out of the Spirit-filled life is love, joy, peace, long-suffering, gentleness, goodness, faithfulness, meekness, and self-control.

As I was writing these lessons, I ran across an old booklet in my husband's library. The following thoughts from that book have kept me going when I am tired and question, "Is it really worth the struggle?"

> "How far up toward the height of His perfect surrender will you climb? He will meet you where you meet Him. The only limit to His fullness is that which you impose in the limitation of your surrender. The more absolutely, sweepingly, irrevocably you yield yourself, time, talents, possessions, plans, hopes, aspirations, purposes, yea all to Jesus Christ, vouching yourself His loving bond-slave to do and suffer His will, the more you shall know the blessed fullness of His Spirit. You may have all the fullness you will make room for. In a profound sense it rests with you. What a tremendous thought! To go through all the long years of life with the privilege, peace, and power of the blessed life within your grasp at any hour and yet to have missed it!"[1]

If you are not perfect yet—but desire to become more like the Perfect One, Jesus Christ—this book can be a great help to you. My prayer is that it will be used of God to transform your life so you will daily see the fruit of the Spirit blossoming in your life.

Note:
1. James H. McConkey, *The Threefold Secret of the Holy Spirit* (Lincoln, NE: Back to the Bible Publishers, 1897), pp. 43, 44.

PART 1

TILLING THE SOIL WHERE THE FRUIT WILL GROW

Nine lessons in this Bible study deal with the fruit of the Spirit as listed in Galatians 5:22 and 23. However, before we look at each of these qualities individually, we need to prepare the soil in which the fruit will grow. Before a farmer can grow a good crop, he must prepare the soil by tilling, or breaking, the hard lumps. The soil we are talking about is our heart. The fruit of the Spirit grows best and flourishes more easily in a prepared heart. Lessons 1 through 3 of this study will help us till the soil of our heart.

LESSON 1

Why Do I Keep Sinning?

"Likewise reckon ye also yourselves to be dead indeed unto sin, but alive unto God through Jesus Christ our Lord"
(Romans 6:11).

Which would you rather have in your life: ugly sins or beautiful spiritual fruit? The choice is yours! We will learn in this lesson that we are dead to sin. That means we no longer have to sin. We sin now because we *choose* to sin. Remember, THE CHOICE IS YOURS! Which will it be: ugly sins or spiritual fruit?

The *New York Times* once reported that a man had returned to his home in Wales after having lived in New York City for thirty-four years. He had come to the United States to find employment, and eventually he quit writing his family in Wales. After seven years a Welsh court declared him dead, so his wife legally remarried. When the man returned to Wales, he found that he had thirteen grandchildren and eleven great-grandchildren. Thus a man returned home—legally dead, but very much alive!

There is quite a difference between being dead and being legally dead. Triumphant Christian living begins with an understanding of the fact that every Christian is, in the sight of God, legally dead!

1. The Bible gives a vivid picture of us before we were born again and alive unto God. What is that picture according to Ephesians 2:1?

2. What does "dead in trespasses and sins" mean?

3. What contrast is pictured in Ephesians 2:1 and Romans 6:2?

Ephesians 2:1—Before salvation:

Romans 6:2— After salvation:

"Just as you believed at first that He delivered you from the guilt of sin because He said it, so now believe that He delivers you from the power of sin because He says it. . . . Just as much as He came to deliver you from future punishment did He also come to deliver you from present bondage."[1]

To understand the picture of death to sin, we must see it from two sides: the positional side and the practical side.

POSITIONAL SIDE

Legally: We are dead in God's sight.

Galatians 2:20—We are crucified with Christ.

Romans 6:3, 4—We are baptized, or placed, into His death.

Romans 6:6—Our old man (old nature) is crucified with Him.

Positionally: We are freed from sin's power.

PRACTICAL SIDE

Experientially: We are alive in men's sight.

1 John 1:8—If we say we have no sin, we deceive ourselves.

Romans 7:15–25—Paul constantly battled the flesh, the sin principle.

Galatians 5:17—We, like Paul, battle daily with the flesh.

Practically: We still struggle with sin.

Satan was once the authority who ruled our lives; He was our master. We sinned because we were spiritually dead and lacked the power not to sin. But that is no longer true. When we are born again (John 3:3–7), we become new creations in Christ (1 Corinthians 5:17). We are to walk in newness of life (Romans 6:4). We are legally dead to sin.

4. Death is separation. Since we are legally dead in Christ, from what are we separated? Read Romans 6:7.

5. Since a believer is freed from the power of sin, why does she still have such a struggle with sin? Read Colossians 3:9 and 10 and Ephesians 4:22–24.

"Christian, what hast thou to do with sin? Hath it not cost thee enough already? Burnt child, wilt thou play with fire? . . . Hast thou not had enough of the old serpent? . . . Did sin ever yield thee real pleasure? Didst thou find solid satisfaction in it? If so, go back to thine old drudgery, and wear the chain again, if it delight thee."[2]

How can we gain control over the flesh, which no longer has any right to rule us but continues to try? Paul explains how we can gain control in Romans 6:1–13. As we study these verses, we sense he is challenging us in our intellect, emotions, and will.

Intellect: "Know ye" (verse 3)

6. After reading Romans 6:1–13, describe how verse 3 involves our intellect.

"I am in Christ and identified with Him. Therefore, whatever happened to Christ has happened to me. When He died, I died. When He arose, I arose in Him. I am now seated with Him in the heavenlies! (see Eph. 2:1-10; Col. 3:1-3) Because of this living union with Christ, the believer has a totally new relationship to sin."[3]

Emotions: "Reckon ye" (verse 11)

7. The Greek word for "reckon" *(igizomai)* means "to count" or "to take into account." How are our emotions involved when we take into account that the Bible says we are dead to sin, or freed from sin's power?

Will: "Yield yourselves" (verse 13)

8. How is the will involved in yielding one's self to God?

9. If we don't have to sin anymore, why do we? Read James 1:13–15.

10. When we were crucified with Christ, we became legally dead to sin. What other dramatic change took place in our lives? Read Galatians 2:20.

11. The following passages reveal that Christ lives in us: 1 Corinthians 6:19; Romans 8:9, 10. How does Christ live in us?

12. Romans 8:2 calls the Holy Spirit "the Spirit of life in Christ Jesus." What exciting and significant truth does this verse teach?

13. Have you ever thought about the fact that the struggle with sin is often more difficult after salvation than before? Why is this so? Read Romans 7:15–25.

> *"The believer has an old nature that wants to keep him in bondage; 'I will get free from these old sins!' the Christian says to himself. 'I determine here and now that I will not do this any longer.' What happens? He exerts all his willpower and energy, and for a time succeeds; but then when he least expects it, he falls again. Why? . . . If we depend on the energy of the flesh, we cannot serve God, please God, or do any good thing. But if we yield to the Holy Spirit, then we have the power needed to obey His will. The flesh will never serve the Law of God because the flesh is at war with God. But the Spirit can only obey the Law of God!"[4]*

This list gives the deeds of the flesh as recorded in Galatians 5:19–21. These are sins a Christian can commit when she chooses to yield to the enticements of the flesh.

Adultery: Illicit sex between married people

Fornication: Illicit sex between unmarried people

Uncleanness: Filthiness of heart and mind

Lasciviousness: Indecent, unrestrained, and shameless conduct

Idolatry: Anything that comes ahead of God in one's life

Sorcery (witchcraft): Involvement in occult practices

Hatred: Holding bitterness and anger toward others

Strife (variance): Causing division and discord

Jealousy (emulations): Rivalries; trying to make someone look bad in the eyes of another

Wrath: Uncontrolled anger

Factions (strife): Debating contentiously with enmity; divisions

Seditions: Causing dissension by false teaching

Heresies: Self-willed opinions contrary to Scripture

Envyings: Wrongful desires to possess what belongs to another

Murders: Destroying another person; taking another person's life by deed or thought

Drunkenness: Being under the control of intoxicating drink or drugs

Revelings: Uncontrolled rioting and pleasure-making; drunken carousings

And the like: The list continues indefinitely

14. The deeds of the flesh could be put into four categories. How would you label each of these groups?
(a) Immorality, impurity, sensuality: _____

(b) Idolatry, sorcery: _____

(c) Strife, jealousy, wrath, envyings: _____

(d) Drunkenness, revelings: _____

15. How can we yield to the Holy Spirit's control rather than to the control of the flesh? Read Galatians 5:24.

16. How can we crucify the flesh? Read Romans 6:17 and 18.

17. Read Romans 12:1. What does it mean to "present your bodies a living sacrifice"?

18. Have you ever presented yourself to God and given up your rights, plans, and desires by exchanging your will for His will? If your answer is yes, describe the experience.

If your answer is no, are you willing to do that right now and pray the following prayer?

"Here, Lord, I abandon myself to thee. I have tried in every way I could think of to manage myself, and to make myself what I know I ought to be, but have always failed. Now I give it up to thee. Do thou take entire possession of me. Work in me all the good pleasure of thy will. Mold and fashion me into such a vessel as seemeth good to thee. I leave myself in thy hands, and I believe thou wilt, according to thy promise, make me into a vessel unto thy own honor, 'sanctified, and meet for the master's use, and prepared unto every good work.' "[5]

19. How can we know whether the flesh or the Holy Spirit controls our life? Read Galatians 5:16, 22, and 23.

We must be emptied of self before we can be filled with the Spirit! This is a daily process of emptying and filling—sanctification—if we desire to live the Christlike life.

 ### *From My Heart*

I once read that most Christians have just enough religion to bug them instead of bless them. How true! For many people, the Christian life is a vicious cycle of sinning and confessing their sin, sinning and confessing again. Why is this? Could it be that these people have not heard and understood what Christ has done for them? Christ died not only to set us free from the penalty of sin in the future (Hell), but also to set us free from the power of sin now (Satan's bondage).

I no longer *have* to sin; I sin now because I *choose* to do so. I don't have to yield to God either; that is another choice I must make.

Why have I chosen to yield myself to God? I have learned by experience that the benefits far outweigh choosing to sin.

When I yield myself to God, I have a Captain to fight my battles for me. I have a Burden-bearer to lighten my load through life. I have a Fortress to hide me from the enemy. I have a Shield to protect me, a Guide to lead me, a Comforter to console me, and a Shepherd to care for me.

What about you? Are you making good choices?

From Your Heart

Are you living with a sin that dominates your life? Has Satan deceived you into thinking you can never be free from it? What is that sin? What steps are you going to take to enjoy the freedom that is available to you?

Notes:

1. Hannah Whitall Smith, *The Christian's Secret of a Happy Life* (Westwood, NJ: Fleming H. Revell Co., 1952), p. 53.

2. Charles H. Spurgeon, *Morning and Evening* (Lynchburg, VA: The Old-Time Gospel Hour, n.d.), p. 303.

3. Warren W. Wiersbe, *The Bible Exposition Commentary,* vol. 1 (Wheaton, IL: Victor Books, 1989), p. 531.

4. Wiersbe, pp. 537, 538.

5. Smith, p. 39.

LESSON 2

What Does the Bible Say about Self-esteem?

"In lowliness of mind let each esteem other better than themselves" (Philippians 2:3).

If we are legally dead to sin and we don't have to sin anymore, why in the world do we keep choosing to sin? We keep sinning because we are self-centered. Self-centeredness is at the root of all those ugly sins listed in Galatians 5:19–21. When we take our eyes off ourselves, we can begin to live an others-centered life. Then all the beautiful fruit in Galatians 5:22 and 23 will begin to blossom in our lives.

We concluded lesson 1 with the statement, "We must be emptied of self before we can be filled with the Spirit." Can we be filled with self-love and deny self simultaneously? The world says, "Love self"; God says, "Deny self." What is influencing our thinking: the philosophy of this world or God's Word?

The world says, "You must learn to love yourself; accept yourself; you deserve better; make sure your needs are met so you have good self-esteem."

God says, "If any man come to me, and hate not . . . his own life also, he cannot be my disciple" (Luke 14:26); "If any man will come after me, let him deny himself, and take up his cross, and follow me" (Matthew 16:24; also Mark 8:34 and Luke 9:23).

How do self-love and self-denial fit together? Or do they? After much study, I have come to the conclusion they cannot fit together. You must accept one teaching or the other. You must accept either what the world is teaching or what God is teaching.

1. Look up the words "self-love" and "self-esteem" in a dictionary. Write the definitions on page 18.

17

Self-love

Self-esteem

2. Using a Bible concordance, make a list of verses that refer to self-love and self-esteem.

3. The Bible never tells us to love ourselves or have a high esteem for ourselves. What does it tell us? Read Philippians 2:3 and 4 and Luke 14:26.

4. Self-love advocates say we must learn to love ourselves because we cannot love God and others until we first learn to love ourselves. What does God say? Does He say we must learn to love ourselves, or does He say we already love ourselves? Read Ephesians 5:28, 29; Philippians 2:21; 2 Timothy 3:2.

ALL WRAPPED UP IN ME, MYSELF, AND I
I love me. I love to hear you talk about me. I view myself continually in what you say about me. I expect to be appreciated. I am sensitive to slights. I never forgive a criticism. I trust no one but myself. I demand you agree with me on everything.

    One of the world's most unattractive packages is a person all wrapped up in himself.

---

5. The world says a person with a poor self-image needs to learn to love herself when the truth is we really love ourselves too much. The very sin at the core of our lives is pride, self-centeredness. How is pride, or self-centeredness, demonstrated in the life of a person with a poor self-image?

"The original sin, pride, is behind my 'poor self-image,' for I felt that I deserved better than I got, which is exactly what Eve felt! So it was pride, not poor self-image, that had to go. If I'm so beautiful and lovable, what was Jesus doing up there, nailed and crowned with thorns? Why all that hideous suffering for the pure Son of God? Here's why: there was no other way to deliver us from the hell of our own proud self-loving selves, no other way out of the bondage of self-pity and self-congratulation."[1]

---

6. Describe how we make ourselves slaves to ourselves.

7. What are some factors that contribute to a low view of self?

8. The fundamental view of self-love, self-esteem supporters is this: a person may realize fulfillment and satisfaction only when her needs for significance and security are being met. Do you know any person or thing on this earth that can meet all your needs for significance and

security? Who alone can do that? Read Philippians 4:19
and Ephesians 3:20.

9. How does Christ meet our need for security?
   Jeremiah 31:3

   1 John 1:9

   Psalm 139:1–4

10. How does Christ meet our need for significance?
    Matthew 25:21

    Hebrews 13:5

    Matthew 25:35–40

   It requires human design and engineering to make a
mirror so we can look at ourselves. God's design was for
man to look upward and outward—not at self.

11. Describe the contrast between God's love, *agape* love,
    and self-love. Read 1 Corinthians 13:4–8.

> *"Well-meaning therapists had discussed my problems [depression and emotional instability] with me many times before, but the root of my need had never been exposed and dealt with. God began to show me the revolting root of 'self' in my life, with all of its many faces—self-pity, self-introspection, self-condemnation, self-centeredness, self-defense, and on and on the list went. Self, self, self—that's what was at the root of my damaged mental and emotional condition.*
>
> *Instead of humbling myself before God and embracing the opportunity to cry out for His grace (the desire and the power to respond God's way), I had responded to the storms of life by holding onto and pampering my self—my hurts, my disappointments, my rights, my needs.*
>
> *What a release it was to acknowledge that the circumstances of my past had not made me what I was; they had simply revealed the deep root of self that needed to be taken to the cross, so that I could exchange my bitter, unforgiving self for the loving, sacrificial, forgiving Life of Jesus."[2]*

12. Can a person whose own self-love needs have not been met or a person who had a terrible life as a child ever learn to express the *agape* love described in 1 Corinthians 13:4–8? If so, how? Read 2 Corinthians 5:17 and 2 Peter 1:3.

13. The apostle Paul was deprived of many things after he came to know Christ as His Savior. He didn't have people stroking him and telling him how valuable he was, how loved and accepted he was. What did people do to Paul? Read 2 Corinthians 6:4–10; 11:23–28.

14. How could such a "deprived person" love God and others and feel he was a profitable servant for God? Read Philippians 4:11–13.

"The weakest saint can experience the power of the Deity of the Son of God if once he is willing to 'let go.' Any strand of our own energy will blur the life of Jesus. We have to keep letting go, and slowly and surely the great full life of God will invade us in every part, and men will take knowledge of us that we have been with Jesus."[3]

---

15. We see no spirit of pride in Paul, no morbid spirit of self-contempt. Paul realized that when the Holy Spirit distributed His gifts, he had not been left out (Romans 12:3, 6–8). Paul knew what his gifts were, but he never claimed personal credit for any virtue or talent. What valuable gifts did Paul recognize he had?
1 Corinthians 3:10

1 Corinthians 4:1

1 Corinthians 4:15, 16

1 Corinthians 15:10

16. If a child of God demands to hang on to her past and use it as an excuse for not being able to love and forgive, what is she actually doing? Read Galatians 5:17–23.

17. How can such a person, in bondage to her past, be set free? Psalm 51:1, 2, 12

2 Peter 1:2–4

Galatians 5:16, 22, 23

18. What is the Biblical alternative for self-love or self-esteem? Read Matthew 16:24 and 25.

19. "Life" and "self" are used interchangeably in Mark 8:34–38, Luke 9:23–25, John 12:25, and Matthew 16:25. What does it mean to "deny self" or "lose your life?"

"Lord, deliver me from the faithless desire for self-preservation when obedience to You requires self-abandonment."[4]

---

20. What does this statement say to you: "I must treat myself, with all my sinful practices, like a criminal"?

21. What is involved in daily denying ourselves? Read Romans 12:1 and 2.

This lesson started with the question, How do self-love and self-denial fit together? Can we be filled with self-love (as the world says we must) and deny self (as God says we must) simultaneously? It is obvious we can't! We must choose one teaching or the other.

The world says, "Look out for self; make sure all your needs are met; you can't love others because you were never loved."

A person who believes this philosophy is stuck with what happened in her past. Low self-esteem takes the blame off the person and places the blame for her sin or troubles on another person or circumstance. The person is helpless until the circumstances change.

The problem is not what happened to us, no matter how painful it may be. The problem is our determination to avoid being hurt again, which leads to a life of self-protection and self-centeredness.

God says, "Live for Me and quit thinking about self" (2 Corinthians 5:15; Romans 14:7, 8). The only escape from loving self is surrendering self.

Are we stuck with what happened to us in the past? No! We can't blame our troubles on low self-esteem if we belong to Jesus Christ. "Therefore if any man be in Christ, he is a new creature: old things are passed away; behold, all things are become new" (2 Corinthians 5:17). Our sinful methods of reacting to the sinful behavior of others can be replaced by love, joy, peace, long-suffering, gentleness, goodness, faith, meekness, and self-control (Galatians 5:22, 23). When we begin to see ourselves as God sees us, we will be amazed at His evaluation of our worthiness and value.

"A healthy self-image is 'seeing yourself as God sees you—no more and no less.' "[5]

---

22. How does God see us?
    John 1:12

    1 Corinthians 3:16

    Romans 5:10

Romans 5:1

2 Corinthians 5:20

2 Corinthians 5:21

Jeremiah 31:3

What image do you have of yourself in God's eyes?

"Jesus . . . help me to find adventure in my uniqueness, and not want to be what someone else is. God, if i lose sight of the fun of being me, then Your dreams of what i can be in the world will die. always help me to remember that this is Your way of being creative."[6]

 From My Heart

When I wrote my first Bible study, *Trials—Don't Resent Them as Intruders,* I realized I had to write a personal profile. To be honest, I didn't know what to say. So I looked at the profiles on the backs of other books and read what was written about the authors. My first thought was, "Oh my, I don't have any degrees to put behind my name." Then I thought, "Oh, yes, I do: P.W.—Pastor's Wife. Anyone can go to school to earn a degree, but only God can give you that degree."

I heard Zig Ziglar say something that made me realize how unimpressed God may be with all our degrees. He said that knowledge is not the only answer. Many people with great knowledge are absolute failures in life. Wisdom is the answer—the wisdom that comes from God. When we know Christ as our Savior, we have all we need in life.

When we take our knowledge, no matter how limited it

may be, and add to that the spiritual knowledge God wants to give to all His children and add to that God's wisdom (which God promises to give to each of His children who ask for it [James 1:5])—WOW! I realize now I am a special and valuable person.

Even if I didn't put P.W. behind my name, I would still be a person of great worth. Do you know why? For the same reason you are if you belong to Jesus Christ. My feeling of self-worth does not come from whom I know or with whom I am associated on this earth or from my status in life. My self-worth comes from knowing WHO I AM and TO WHOM I BELONG. I know I am a poor helpless sinner, saved by God's wondrous mercy and love for me at Calvary. Who am I? I am a child of the King! To whom do I belong? I belong to the King; I am His child; I am a princess!

As long as you can see yourself as God sees you, you will never have another problem with self-esteem.

I can already hear some of you saying, "That's easy for you to say because you have never been an abused child, divorced, abandoned by your children, or rejected by your family." My answer to you is, "You are right!" However, in more than thirty years as a pastor's wife, I have seen about every form of abuse and suffering. I know scores of ladies who have suffered terrible abuse and pain, but who could write the same things I have just written. I have asked two of my friends to write to you *from their heart* what Christ has done for them.

From the heart of a lady who suffered divorce

My father walked out when I was a baby. I had two alcoholic stepfathers and a retarded brother. I was passed from my mother, two aunts, and periodically to my father. I was saved as a young teenager, and all I desired was a Christian home. I went to Bible college and married another student. We graduated and started serving the Lord. My husband gradually began to let sin come into his life. After twenty-seven years of marriage and two affairs, he left our home and continued his affair.

I had no self-esteem (not low self-esteem, no self-esteem). I felt that I had failed God, my husband, and my children. I felt I must be a terrible person and worth nothing. I had a head full of Bible verses, but they were of no comfort. I used them to try to manipulate God.

God and His Word are faithful. As I stayed in the Word daily and listened to a twenty-four-hour Christian radio station, ever so gradually I started applying God's Word to my life. These verses were especially helpful to me: Jeremiah 29:11; 31:3; Psalms 32:8; 56:3; John 14:18. I began really living the palms-up life Juanita had taught me. [See lesson 6, *Trials—Don't Resent Them as Intruders.*] God used this truth, along with my pastor's godly messages and wise counsel and my church family, to patiently begin to restore my self-esteem.

After eight years of separation, my husband divorced me and was remarried within a couple of days. Now, I humbly thank the Lord for what He has done and is still doing in my life. He does love me, and I know I am worth more than silver, gold, and rubies because He died for me. I want Him to mold me, take away the dross and use me as I continue to learn to live the palms-up life. My self-esteem now comes from the realization of what God has done and is doing in my life.

From the heart of a lady who suffered sexual abuse

"Your father does not love you; he never even wanted you." That was what Grandma told me. As a result of that apparent rejection, I was easy prey for sexual abuse. I was sexually abused for years by one whom I was taught to love and respect. He even passed me around for his friends to enjoy. Oh, the devastation I felt when I was old enough to realize what had happened to me. For many years I felt of no value to anyone and considered myself ugly, dirty, unloved, and not at all worthy of love.

God broke that vicious pattern of thinking when I understood Christ loved me and that He died for my sin. I was overwhelmed to know God's love and forgiveness.

After Christ saved me, many changes were needed in my life to overcome years of selfish living and thinking. I, like many people who have been abused, tried to find self-worth and self-acceptance by working hard for the approval of others. That did not work, and often I was left rejected and alone.

As I have learned more from God's Word about God's grace and about my own sinful self and selfish motives, God has changed me. I now know the wonderful freedom of being unconditionally loved by God and the real joy of loving and serving others.

My dear friend, if sin has devastated your life, please turn to God's Word and learn of His care. Let Him change your self-centered, hurting life into a Christ-centered, joyful life. Turn your eyes away from self and to the God Who understands the pain of sin but longs to fill your life with His Spirit. He has done it for me, and He will do it for you!

From Your Heart

Has the world's philosophy of self-love affected you in any way? Do you need to correct your thinking regarding self-love and self-denial? Do you have a healthy self-image?

Notes:

1. Elisabeth Elliot Gren, *The Elisabeth Elliot Newsletter* (Ann Arbor, MI: Servant Publications, 1991), July/August 1991 issue.

2. "Free Through Christ," *Spirit of Revival* (June 1992), p. 9.

3. Oswald Chambers, *My Utmost for His Highest* (New York: Dodd, Mead & Co., 1935), p. 103.

4. Elisabeth Elliot, *A Lamp for My Feet* (Ann Arbor, MI: Servant Publications, 1985), p. 39.

5. Josh McDowell, *Building Your Self-Image* (Wheaton, IL: Tyndale House Publishers, Inc., 1984), p. 39.

6. Ann Kiemel, *I Love the Word Impossible* (Wheaton, IL: Tyndale House Publishers, Inc., 1976), p. 107.

LESSON 3

I Want to Be Spiritual Now!

*"And be not drunk with wine, wherein is excess;
but be filled with the Spirit" (Ephesians 5:18).*

If you have applied lessons 1 and 2 to your life, the soil of your heart should be tilled enough for the planting and growing process to begin. But don't forget: this is a *process!* The fruit of the Spirit will not spring up in your heart and life overnight. However, it will begin to grow as you daily water and fertilize your soul with the Word of God.

We cannot become mature, godly women in a day. There is no such thing as instant godliness. However, we can begin the spiritual journey to godliness now. Yes, we can start today! This spiritual journey begins by learning how to live a Spirit-filled life.

In this lesson we will discover how we can live the abundant, Spirit-filled life that God has planned for every child of God. Galatians 5:16 tells us to "walk in the Spirit." How long will it take us to learn to walk in the Spirit? How long does it take a baby to learn to walk? Some babies learn in eight months, some ten months, some one year, and some longer than that. You will not learn to walk in the Spirit in one lesson; it is a daily process. It starts when you take the first step. Just as a child's confidence in walking grows after much stumbling, falling, and getting up again, so it is that we grow in our confidence in God to help us learn to walk in the Spirit.

Who can be filled with the Holy Spirit?
1. After reading John 14:16 and 17, complete this sentence: Today the Holy Spirit dwells _____ .

2. When does the Holy Spirit take up residence in the believer's life? Read Ephesians 1:13 and 14 and 2 Corinthians 5:17.

3. For whom is the filling of the Spirit reserved? Read John 3:3–6; 7:37 and 38.

What does Spirit-filled, or Spirit-controlled, mean?

Does it mean we get more and more of the Holy Spirit, like filling a cup with water until it overflows? No; the Holy Spirit doesn't come in spurts or piecemeal. He is a Person, and we have all of Him the moment we are saved. The filling, or controlling, of the Holy Spirit is the influence the Spirit exercises over us when we yield ourselves totally to His control.

4. What command is given to believers in Ephesians 5:18?

The Holy Spirit resides in each believer's life; however, He does not want to be just resident but PRESIDENT. He wants to control us!

Read Ephesians 5:18–21. People identify a person who is drunk with wine by that person's actions. People will identify a person who is controlled with the Spirit by that person's actions.

A person who is drunk with wine:	A person who is filled with the Spirit:
• walks differently	• walks differently
• talks differently	• talks differently
• acts differently	• acts differently
• thinks differently	• thinks differently
• feels differently	• feels differently
Alcohol's control results in *impaired* judgment	The Spirit's control results in *improved* judgment[1]

How can we be controlled by the Holy Spirit?

Our lives must revolve around four things each day:

(1) Keep a Christ-centered life.
(2) Keep in God's Word.
(3) Keep a yielded, submissive spirit.
(4) Keep saying no to sin and yes to righteousness (doing right).

Keep a Christ-centered life.

5. Read Philippians 3:10–14 and Romans 8:29. Describe a Christ-centered life.

"To be transformed into the image of Christ I must learn his character, love his obedience to the will of the Father, and begin, step by step, to walk the same pathway. For Christ the pathway of obedience began with emptying Himself. I must begin at the same place."[2]

Keep in God's Word.

6. We may know God's Word and hear it taught regularly, but why is it so important to look into the "perfect law of liberty" (God's Word) each day? Read James 1:22–25.

Keep a yielded, submissive spirit.

7. Read Romans 12:1; then jot down your description of a yielded spirit.

"How far up toward the height of His perfect surrender will you climb? He will meet you where you meet Him. The only limit to His fullness is that which you impose in the limitation of your surrender. The more absolutely, sweepingly, irrevocably you yield yourself, time, talents, possessions, plans, hopes, aspirations, purposes, yea all to Jesus Christ, vouching yourself His loving bond-slave to do and suffer His will, the more you shall know the blessed fullness of His Spirit. You may have all the fullness you will make room for. In a profound sense it rests with you. What a tremendous thought! To go through all the long years of life with the privilege, peace, and power of the blessed life within your grasp at any hour and yet to have missed it!"[3]

---

8. In Ephesians 5:18 the statement "be filled" is in the imperative mood, which means it is a command.

(a) Do we have to obey this command? _____
(b) Why will we want to obey it?

9. "Be filled" is also in the present progressive tense, which means it can be translated "keep on being filled." What does that fact suggest about the filling of the Spirit?

Keep saying no to sin and yes to righteousness.
10. How can we "put off" the flesh and reject sin in our lives? Read Ephesians 4:22–24 and Romans 6:1 and 2.

"If a man or woman honestly wishes to be a follower, the opportunity will present itself. Christ will say, 'Here is your chance. Now, in this situation, you must make your choice. Will it be self? Or will you choose Me?'

An older missionary said something to Amy Carmichael when she was a young missionary that stayed with her for life. She had spoken of something which was not to her liking. His reply was, 'See in it a chance to die.' "[4]

How can I tell when I am Spirit-filled?
Ephesians 5:18–21 gives four evidences of Spirit-filling:
  (1) I will be joyful and want fellowship.
  (2) I will have a heart filled with praise.
  (3) I will have a grateful spirit.
  (4) I will have a reverent, submissive spirit toward others.

I will be joyful and want fellowship.
11. How does Ephesians 5:19 express this thought?

I will have a heart filled with praise.
12. (a) Does Ephesians 5:19 mean a person always sings?
_____ (b) What does it mean?

I will have a grateful spirit.
13. Ephesians 5:20 and 1 Thessalonians 5:18 exhort us to give thanks always and for all things. How can we do this when everything seems to be falling apart?

I will have a reverent, submissive spirit toward others.
14. According to Ephesians 5:21, why must reverence for Christ be the source of a submissive spirit?

Further evidence of a Spirit-filled life: spiritual fruit
15. Galatians 5:22 and 23 point out that nine moral qualities called "the fruit of the Spirit" will mark the Spirit-filled person. In the following lessons we will study each of these qualities that the Spirit produces in the yielded child of God. How much do you know about the fruit of the Spirit? In your own words, write a brief description of each quality.
Love

Joy

Peace

Long-suffering

Gentleness

Goodness

Faithfulness (faith)

Meekness

Self-control (temperance)

"The contrast between works *and* fruit *is important. A machine in a factory* works, *and turns out a product, but it could never manufacture fruit. Fruit must grow out of life, and, in the case of the believer, it is the life of the Spirit (Gal. 5:25). . . . The flesh produces 'dead works' (Heb. 9:14), but the Spirit produces living fruit. . . . The old nature cannot produce fruit; only the new nature can do that."*[5]

 From My Heart

If someone asked you, "Is your life Spirit-filled or self-filled?" how would you answer? How should you answer?

Writing this lesson reminded me again that being filled with the Spirit is not an option but a command. I was also reminded that it is a continual process. I must daily be emptied of self and filled with the Spirit.

Christ wants me to have an overflowing, abundant life, full of joy. I am learning that the more I get to know my Savior, the more I know how to avail myself of all the riches He wants to give me. This poem by Nancy Spiegelberg describes my own spiritual journey to godliness. Does it describe your experience as well?

Lord,
I crawled
across the barrenness
to You
with my empty cup,

uncertain
but asking
any small drop
of refreshment.

If only
I had known You better
I'd have come
running with a bucket. [6]

From Your Heart

Have you experienced the Spirit-filled life? Would you like to begin your spiritual journey to godliness today? What four things must you do to get started?

Notes:
1. *How Can I Be Filled with the Holy Spirit?* (Grand Rapids: Radio Bible Class, 1986), p. 9.
2. Elliot, *A Lamp for My Feet,* p. 29.
3. McConkey, pp. 43, 44.
4. Elliot, *A Lamp for My Feet,* p. 30.
5. Wiersbe, p. 719.
6. Nancy Spiegelberg, quoted by Erwin W. Lutzer, *How to Say No to a Stubborn Habit* (Wheaton, IL: Victor Books, 1979), p. 54.

PART 2

RECOGNIZING THE FRUIT AS IT GROWS

Learning to walk in the Spirit is not a pie-in-the-sky dream attained only by age-old saints, Bible teachers, and preachers. Walking in the Spirit is God's desire and plan for every child of His. Before we were saved, our lives were filled with all the ugly, fleshly sins listed in Galatians 5:19–21. Now that we are new creations in Christ (2 Corinthians 5:17), God wants our lives to be filled with all the beautiful fruit listed in Galatians 5:22 and 23. Will the fruit automatically begin to grow in our lives? No! We must learn to walk in the Spirit. As we do this, the fruit of the Spirit will become part of our daily lives. These lessons will help us recognize the fruit as it develops in our heart and is evidenced in our relationships with one another.

LESSON 4

Love—Not a Feeling but a Choice

"By this shall all men know that ye are my disciples, if ye have love one to another" (John 13:35).

Each day I am faced with choices and challenges. Daily I must choose not to sin. Daily I must choose to be emptied of self and filled with the Holy Spirit. Likewise, daily I must choose to love others whether I feel like it or not!

Someone once said, "If we all obeyed the royal law (James 2:8—'Thou shalt love thy neighbour as thyself') there would be no need for any other laws." How true!

As we begin to examine each aspect of the fruit of the Spirit, we will learn that love is the essential ingredient for all the other graces to grow. Joy, peace, long-suffering, gentleness, goodness, meekness, faithfulness, and self-control all stem from love.

We are commanded to love others whether we feel like it or not (1 John 4:20, 21). But it really doesn't make any difference whether we feel like it or not because God's love is not a feeling but an action—A CHOICE! We are commanded to treat others the way Christ treats us (John 15:12). *When I begin to love others the way Christ loves me, I will begin to understand unconditional love.*

1. Most of us do not exemplify God's kind of love in our lives. How is God's love different from ours? Read Jeremiah 31:3.

God's love is unconditional. God loves us no matter what. He has no conditions attached to His love.

2. (a) Do you know someone who practices unconditional

37

love?_____ (b) Do you practice it? _____
(c) If so, describe an incident in your life when you
demonstrated this kind of love.

"Love, to be all that it was meant to be, is non-negotiably unconditional. We extend it even when it costs us something, regardless of return. God's unconditional, inconvenient gift of love through Christ is the ultimate example."[1]

---

3. Often our love is selfish, self-gratifying, and self-protective. What did Christ's love always involve? Read Galatians 2:20.

4. Based on John 15:12, describe how we are to love one another.

5. (a) Is God expecting an utter impossibility of us when He tells us to demonstrate unconditional love toward one another? _____ (b) What will this kind of love involve according to Philippians 2:3–7.

First Corinthians 13:4–8 is a beautiful description of God's love, *agape* love. Christ wants us to have this kind of love for one another. *Agape* love always results in action on our part. Each aspect of *agape* love is described on the following pages. Grade yourself from A to F on how well you exhibit this love in your life. (All descriptions are taken from the Biblical Counseling Foundation's manual, *Self-confrontation.*[2])
    Read 1 Corinthians 13:4–8.

Love suffereth long (v. 4).

"LOVE IS PATIENT, even when you feel like forcefully expressing yourself. Love bears pain or trials without complaint, shows forbearance under provocation or strain, and is steadfast despite opposition, difficulty, or adversity."

My grade: _____

6. Where do we get the patience we need to suffer long with people? Read Isaiah 40:31 and Psalm 91:1, 2, 14, 15.

Love is kind (v. 4).

"LOVE IS KIND, even when you want to retaliate physically or tear down another with your words. Love is sympathetic, considerate, gentle, and agreeable."

My grade: _____

7. Some people are very critical and unkind. Why must we be kind to people like them? Read John 13:34 and 35.

"Frustration, loneliness, self-pity, indifference, emptiness, hostility, hatred, closeheartedness, resentment, jealousy . . . all grow like wild weeds to fill the holes gouged in our hearts when nobody seems to care."[3]

Love envieth not (v. 4).

"LOVE IS NOT JEALOUS, especially when you are aware that others are being noticed more than you. Love does not participate in rivalry, is not hostile toward one believed to enjoy an advantage, and is not suspicious. Love works for the welfare and good of the other."

My grade: _____

8. Read Philippians 2:3–7 and consider how these verses can help us with envy. What is the main thrust of these verses?

Love vaunteth not itself, is not puffed up (v. 4).

"LOVE DOES NOT BRAG, even when you want to tell the world about your accomplishments. Love . . . does not engage in self-glorification. Instead, love lifts (builds up) others.

LOVE IS NOT ARROGANT, even when you think you are right and others are wrong. Love does not . . . become overbearing in dealing with others."

My grade: _____

9. Self-conscious pride can make us look foolish. How can John 3:30 help us?

Love does not behave itself unseemly (v. 5).

"LOVE DOES NOT ACT UNBECOMINGLY, even when being boastful, rude, or overbearing will get you attention and allow you to get your own way. Love conforms to what is right, fitting, and appropriate to the situation in order to honor the Lord."

My grade: _____

10. To whom are we most likely to be rude and discourteous?

> Able to suffer without complaining;
> To be misunderstood without explaining;
>
> Able to give without receiving,
> To be ignored without grieving;
>
> Able to ask without commanding,
> To love despite misunderstanding;
>
> Able to turn to the Lord for guarding;
> Able to wait for His own rewarding.[4]

Love seeketh not her own (v. 5).

"LOVE DOES NOT SEEK ITS OWN, even when you feel like grabbing it all or have an opportunity to do so. Love does not try to fulfill its own desires, does not ask for its own way, and does not try to acquire gain for itself. Love, as an act of the will, seeks to serve not be served."

My grade: _____

11. Galatians 6:2 instructs us to bear one another's burdens. Why do we not have many burden-bearers today?

> Love this world through me, Lord
> This world of broken men,
> Thou didst love through death, Lord
> Oh, love in me again!
> Souls are in despair, Lord.
> Oh, make me know and care;
> When my life they see,
> May they behold Thee,
> Oh, love the world through me.[5]

Love is not easily provoked (v. 5).

"LOVE IS NOT PROVOKED, even when others attempt to provoke you or you are tempted to strike out at something or someone. Love is not aroused or incited to outbursts of anger. Love continues faithfully and gently to train others in righteousness, even when they fail."

My grade: _____

12. (a) What are we prone to use as an excuse for our bad temper?

(b) Where should we place the blame?

Love thinketh no evil (v. 5).

"LOVE DOES NOT TAKE INTO ACCOUNT A WRONG SUFFERED, even when everyone seems to be against you or when people openly attack you. Love does not hold a grudge against someone. Love forgives, chooses not to bring up past wrongs in accusation or retaliation, does not return evil for evil, and does not indulge in self-pity. Love covers a multitude of sins."

My grade: _____

13. (a) When you are having trouble forgiving and forgetting, what do you need to do with your mind? Read Isaiah 26:3.

(b) What can you think on?

"Since love is an emotion regulated by the lover, not the one being loved, then it is possible for one to love everybody, even enemies. Actually, it is more than a possibility; it is a definite command given by Jesus: 'But I say unto you, Love your enemies, Bless them that curse you, Do good to them that hate you, And pray for them which despitefully use you and persecute you.' Matthew 5:44."[6]

Love rejoiceth not in iniquity (v. 6).

"LOVE DOES NOT REJOICE IN UNRIGHTEOUSNESS, *even when it seems like a misfortune was exactly what another person deserved.* Love mourns over sin, its effects, and the pain which results from living in a fallen world. Love seeks to reconcile others with the Lord."

My grade: _____

14. How are we ever able to love our enemies? Read Matthew 5:44–48 and James 4:17.

Love rejoiceth in the truth (v. 6).

"LOVE REJOICES WITH THE TRUTH, *even when it is easier and more profitable materially to lie.* Love is joyful when truth is known, even when it may lead to adverse circumstances, reviling, or persecution."

My grade: _____

15. Why is it not always easy for us to tell the truth or do what is right? Read Matthew 10:34–38.

Love beareth all things (v. 7).

"LOVE BEARS ALL THINGS, *even when disappointments seem overwhelming.* Love is tolerant, endures with others who are difficult to understand or deal with, and has an eternal perspective in difficulties. Love remembers that God develops spiritual maturity through difficult circumstances."

My grade: _____

16. When difficult trials come, what gives us the courage to bear them and not run from them? Read James 1:2–4.

Love believeth all things (v. 7).

"LOVE BELIEVES ALL THINGS, even when others' actions are ambiguous and you feel like not trusting anyone. Love accepts trustfully, does not judge people's motives, and believes others until facts prove otherwise. Even when facts prove that the person is untrustworthy, love seeks to help restore the other to trustworthiness."

My grade: _____

17. How can you keep believing someone who has lied to you and continues to lie?

Love hopeth all things (v. 7).

"LOVE HOPES ALL THINGS, even when nothing appears to be going right. Love expects fulfillment of God's plan and anticipates the best for the other person. Love confidently entrusts others to the Lord to do His sovereign and perfect will in their lives."

My grade: _____

18. When a person is living in sin and the situation looks hopeless, how can Psalm 32:1 encourage us?

"He promises to be bigger than any impossibility
*   because He is love . . .*
*   and love always finds a way through,*
*   in time.*
love isn't scared.
it builds bridges instead of walls.
it never gives up.
it always hangs on.
it waits with stubborn, strong hope.
*   sometimes even years."*[7]

Love endureth all things (v. 7).

"LOVE ENDURES ALL THINGS, especially when you think you just can't stand it anymore with people or circumstances. Love remains steadfast under suffering or hardship without yielding and returns a blessing while undergoing trials."

My grade: _____

19. What can we learn from Christ about enduring mistreatment? Read 1 Peter 2:23.

Love never faileth (v. 8).

"LOVE NEVER FAILS, even when you feel like 'you've had enough' and the situation seems hopeless. Love will not crumble under pressure or difficulties. Love remains selflessly faithful even to the point of death."

My grade: _____

20. Remember Jeremiah 31:3? What kind of love do we demonstrate when God's love is controlling our lives?

God commands us to love others and that includes our enemies and the unlovely. Is this an impossibility? Even with God's help and strength, can we ever love *everybody?* God's love is not a feeling, but an action. It is a choice. We are commanded to treat others the way Christ treats us (John 15:12). Christian love is an action, an act of the will. *We will to treat others the way Christ treats us.*

"You can learn to love, even though you begin with little or no emotional impetus. In other words, you can choose to love. And God gives you the grace to do so.

Love is not an emotion; neither is forgiveness. The Bible commands us to put bitterness away; we are to forgive others whether they solicit our forgiveness or not. Yet many Christians believe that they can't forgive until they feel like it! They think that if they forgive when they don't feel like it, they are hypocritical.

However, if forgiveness were an emotion, God would be commanding you to do the impossible.

*You know that you cannot switch your emotions on
and off. You cannot develop the right feelings on your
own. But God is not mocking you when He tells you to
forgive; you can choose to do so, whether you feel like
it or not. Never try to skirt God's commands under the
pretense that you don't feel like obeying Him."*[8]

 ## *From My Heart*

Those of you who know me know I love to play tennis,
or maybe I should say, "I like to play tennis." As I was writing this lesson, I realized that tennis is similar to life. In
tennis, love means nothing; in other words, I have no points.
In life, love means nothing to many people; they have no
idea what real love is all about. In tennis, when you serve
well, you seldom lose the game. In life, when you serve
others well, you seldom come out a loser.

I am learning that the key to experiencing and expressing God's love in my life is forgetting self and serving others.
WHAT DOES LOVE LOOK LIKE? LOVE LOOKS LIKE JESUS!

From Your Heart

Have you come to the realization that love is a choice
not a feeling. Do you realize you must love whether you feel
like it or not? What steps will you take to let your actions be
regulated by God's Word and not by your feelings? Will you
make a commitment to read 1 Corinthians 13:4–8 daily for
thirty days and ask God to make it a reality in your life?

Notes:

1. Joseph M. Stowell, *Family Happiness Is Homemade* (Vol. 15, No. 8, August 1991), p. 1.

2. John C. Broger, *Self-confrontation* (Rancho Mirage, CA: Biblical Counseling Foundation, 1978), lesson 13, pp. 4–6.

3. George Sweeting, *Love Is the Greatest* (Chicago: Moody Press, 1974), p. 13.

4. Sweeting, p. 54.

5. Will Houghton, quoted by Sweeting, p. 25.

6. Leroy Brownlow, *The Fruit of the Spirit* (Fort Worth: Brownlow Publishing Co., 1982, 1989), p. 15.

7. Kiemel, p. 12.

8. Lutzer, p. 89.

LESSON 5

Joy—Unaffected by People or Circumstances

"In thy presence is fulness of joy; at thy right hand there are pleasures for evermore" (Psalm 16:11).

When I begin to love others the way Christ loves me, I will begin to understand unconditional love. This unconditional love will *bring a supernatural joy into my heart. This joy is not necessarily seen on the face. This joy is a smile of the soul that is unaffected by people or circumstances.*

Love is the stem of the branch from which all the other fruit grows. We will also discover that each aspect of the fruit of the Spirit depends upon the previous fruit. Joy grows out of love. When the love of God flows through our lives, the overflowing joy of Christ will also be evident in our lives.

Jesus said, "I am come that they [His children] might have life, and that they might have it more abundantly" (John 10:10). Christ came to give us not only eternal life in Heaven but also an abundant life here on earth, a life full of joy.

1. We can't wait until everything is going right to be joyful; that may never happen. What command does God give about being joyful? Read 1 Thessalonians 5:16 and Philippians 4:4.

2. What should a Christian do to always be able to rejoice? Read John 15:4, 5, 10, and 11 and Psalm 16:11.

One with Christ, oh, joy divine!
I am His and He is mine.
Oh, the wonder of His grace!
He is my abiding place.
One with Christ 'til life is o'er,
One with Christ forever more.

3. The following verses contain great truths about God. How can these truths help us be joyful?
Psalm 34:8

Psalm 145:17

Jeremiah 31:3

Hebrews 13:5 and 6

4. Many people are concerned about happiness. (a) What is the difference between joy and happiness?

(b) What is the difference between joy and peace?

"Happi-ness *is caused by things which* happen *around me, and circumstances will mar it, but joy flows right on through trouble; joy flows on through the dark; joy flows in the night as well as in the day;*

*joy flows all through persecution and opposition; it
is an unceasing fountain bubbling up in the heart; a
secret spring which the world can't see and doesn't
know anything about. The Lord gives His people
perpetual joy when they walk in obedience to Him."[1]*

5. God promises a heavenly joy, a sacred delight; but this
joy is not cheap. What will it cost us? Read Romans 12:1.

6. This surrendered life could be called the "palms-up" life.
What do you think this term means?

*"Whatever . . . the particular sacrifice God asks you
to make, . . . will you rise up, and say in your heart,
'Yes, Lord, I accept it; I submit, I yield, I pledge
myself to walk in that path, and to follow that Voice,
and to trust Thee with the consequences'? Oh! but
you say, 'I don't know what He will want next.' No,
we none of us know that, but we know we shall be
safe in His hands."[2]*

7. Life is often filled with stress, conflicts, and anxiety. Why
do these things rob us of joy? Read Psalm 16:11.

8. We can allow other people to rob us of joy, but often we
rob ourselves. How do we do this? Read Psalm 51:1 and 2.

*"If you have no joy in your religion, there's a leak
in your Christianity somewhere."[3]*

9. David didn't lose his salvation when he sinned, but he did lose the joy of his salvation (Psalm 51:12). What does it mean to lose the joy of salvation?

10. Sin robs us of joy. How can joy be restored? Read Psalm 51:3 and 4 and 1 John 1:9.

11. What circumstance or person in your life is making it difficult for you to experience the joy of the Lord in your life?

12. Read the verses listed below. How can you experience joy even if the circumstance or person doesn't change? Nehemiah 8:10

    2 Corinthians 12:9 and 10

"The art of life consists in taking each event which befalls us with a contented mind, confident of good. This makes us grow younger as we grow older, for youth and joy come from the soul to the body more than from the body to the soul. With this method and art and temper of life, we live, though we may be dying. We rejoice always, though in the midst of sorrows; and possess all things, though destitute of everything."[4]

---

13. List several "robbers of joy" we might face.

14. On the positive side, what are some "joy givers" that many people enjoy?

     I have learned that even though I go through a dark valley or pass through dismal days, I can have joy in the midst of my trials. These three points have helped me keep the joy of the Lord in my life during difficult days:

> • Get your eyes off your circumstances and on the Lord.
> • Live one day at a time.
> • Count your blessings.

15. How do Isaiah 26:3 and Psalm 1:2 help us know how to get our eyes off people and circumstances and on the Lord?

16. What do the following verses teach us about living one day at a time—just today?
    Philippians 3:13 and 14

    Philippians 4:6 and 7

"Too many of us fix our eyes on our problems — the hurdles—and we start measuring the height of the next jump. In so doing, we glance occasionally at the Lord only to make sure He's aware of all the hardships these hurdles are causing us."[5]

---

17. In what circumstances should we count our blessings? Read 1 Thessalonians 5:18.

18. We can be joyful Christians or joyless Christians; the choice is ours. Describe what you think the joy of the Lord looks like.

19. Someone once said, "Joy is the smile of the soul, and peace is serenity in the soul." Do you know someone who has the "smile of the soul" in his or her life, someone whose life is filled with the joy of the Lord? Describe that person.

20. Think of the most miserable, unhappy Christian you know. Fill out the two columns below with that person in mind.

List the character traits that make her (him) so difficult to be around.	List the traits that the person could exhibit if the joy of the Lord was in her (his) heart.

"Our Christianity is apt to be a very 'dutiful' kind. We mean to do our duty, we attend church and go to our communions. But our hearts are full of the difficulties, the hardships, the obstacles which the situation presents, and we go on our way sadly, downhearted and despondent. We need to learn that true Christianity is inseparable from deep joy; and the secret of that joy lies in a continual looking away from all else . . . to God, His love, His purpose, His will. In proportion as we do look up to Him we shall rejoice, and in proportion as we rejoice in the Lord will our religion have tone and power and attractiveness."[6]

From My Heart

The joy of the Lord should make a difference in my life. If Christ doesn't make a difference in my life, why would anyone want my Savior? People watch me. What do they see?

I heard of a headmaster in a boarding school in London, England, who must have been an unusually godly man. He had such a joyful countenance that one child thought the headmaster could get such joy only by checking into Heaven each night. One day someone asked the headmaster why he was so joyful. He responded with a most amazing statement: "Joy is the flag that is flown from the castle of your heart when the King is in residence." Everyone who lives in London knows that, when Queen Elizabeth is at home, a flag flies over Buckingham Palace.

The kind of joy the headmaster had is determined by whether or not Christ the King is at home in your heart. What about it, ladies? Is Christ at home in your heart? Are you maintaining a close relationship with Him? Remember: Happiness depends on happenings; joy depends on our relationship with Jesus Christ.

The choice is ours. We can have joy if we want it.

From Your Heart

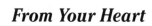

Have you learned you can have joy in your life even if people or circumstances don't change? What must you do? Are you willing to do what you know you should do? What will be the result if you don't do it (James 4:17)?

Notes:

1. Emma Moody Fitt, compiler, *Daily Gems* (Chicago: Moody Press, n.d.), p. 82.

2. Catherine Booth, quoted by Mary Wilder Tileston, compiler, *Joy and Strength* (Minneapolis: World Wide Publications, 1929), p. 44.

3. Billy Sunday, quoted by John Blanchard, compiler, *Gathered Gold* (Durham, England: Evangelical Press, 1984), p. 176.

4. James Freeman Clarke, quoted by Tileston, p. 180.

5. Joni Eareckson Tada, *Seeking God* (Brentwood, TN: Wolgemuth & Hyatt, 1991), p. 135.

6. Charles Gore, quoted by Tileston, p. 252.

LESSON 6

Peace—Living without Worry or Fear

"Thou wilt keep him in perfect peace, whose mind is stayed on thee: because he trusteth in thee" (Isaiah 26:3).

When I begin to love others the way Christ loves me, I will begin to understand unconditional love. This unconditional love will *bring an unexplainable peace to my soul, a serenity that allows me to live without worry or fear. The life that overflows with love and joy will also experience "the peace of God, which passeth all understanding" (Philippians 4:7).*

This peace is something every Christian can have because it is a fruit of the Spirit. However, it is not easy to maintain this peace because of our constant struggle with worry, fear, disappointment, and other pressures. The Lord told us our journey on earth would be filled with trials and persecution, so He gave us 366 "fear not" verses to help us have peace. Just think of that: 366 "fear not" verses, one for each day of the year, even leap year!

Someone once said, "Peace is the conscious possession of adequate resources." We have all the resources we need in God's Word to have peace with God, the peace of God (personal peace), and peace with others. Let's see how this peace is possible.

Peace with God

We receive peace *with* God at the time we are saved.

1. How does the Bible picture the sinner before he is saved? Read Isaiah 57:20 and 21 and Romans 3:17.

2. Describe how a person can have peace with God. Read Ephesians 2:13 and 14 and Romans 5:1.

3. Are you a restless, troubled person with no peace? Would you like to have peace with God? If your answer is yes, you can pray something like this: "Lord Jesus, I know that I am a sinner and need Your forgiveness. I believe You died for my sins. Right now I open the door of my life and receive You as my Savior and Lord. Take control of my life; replace all the restlessness and anxiety with Your joy and peace. Make me the kind of person You want me to be." Share with someone what you have done so that person can help you grow in your newfound faith in Christ.

> *"There is no thirst of the soul so consuming as the desire for pardon. . . . To be able to look into God's face, and know with the knowledge of faith that there is nothing between the soul and Him, is to experience the fullest peace the soul can know. Whatever else pardon may be, it is above all things admission into full fellowship with God."[1]*

The Peace of God

The peace *of* God is the peace God provides for living the Christian life.

4. Once we are God's children and have peace *with* Him, He tells us we can have the peace *of* God. Who gives this peace? Read Philippians 4:7.

5. How would you define the peace of God?

6. Can we have this peace all the time, or is it reserved for times of anxiety and crisis? Read Isaiah 26:3 and explain your answer.

When each earthly prop gives under,
And life seems a restless sea,
Are you then a God-kept wonder,
Satisfied and calm and free?[2]

7. Have you found the key to having peace in your heart?
   What is your plan?

8. What do you learn from Colossians 3:15 about experiencing
   the peace of God?

9. When are you the most likely to lose the peace of God in
   your life?

10. What may cause you to be filled with anxiety instead of
    peace at this time?

11. Many things can rob us of peace, but I think worry and
    fear are two of the most common thieves. (a) What sorts
    of things cause you to worry?

    (b) What sorts of things strike fear in your heart?

"He's the Black Bart of the soul. He doesn't want
your money. He doesn't want your diamonds. He

won't go after your car. He wants something far more precious. He wants your peace of mind— your joy.

His name?

Fear

. . . He doesn't want you to make the journey to the mountain. He figures if he can rattle you enough, you will take your eyes off the peaks and settle for a dull existence in the flatlands."[3]

12. Someone has determined that only 8 percent of the things we worry about ever happen. What are we saying to God when we worry? Read Matthew 6:25–30.

"To be perfectly at peace amid the hurly-burly of daily life is a secret worth knowing. What is the use of worrying? It never made anybody strong; never helped anybody to do God's will; never made a way of escape for anyone out of perplexity. Worry spoils lives which would otherwise be useful and beautiful. Restlessness, anxiety, and care are absolutely forbidden by our Lord, who said: 'Take no thought,' that is, no anxious thought, 'saying what shall we eat, or what shall we drink, or wherewithal shall we be clothed?' "[4]

13. Sometimes we feel as if God has forgotten us and we have no one to help us. How does Matthew 10:29–31 prove this feeling is not true?

14. If Christ knows about and is concerned about even the smallest details of our lives—including the number of hairs on our head—then why do we worry? (Max Factor of Hollywood once hired a person to count the number of hairs on a lady's head. The count was 135,168.)

15. What do Philippians 4:6 and 7 say we must do to have the peace of God ruling in our hearts?
    (a) We must not _____
    (b) We must _____
    (c) We must _____
    (d) Then we will have _____

Peace with Others

Peace with others does not need to be defined; we know what it means. What we do need to know is how we can practice it. If you do not have peace with God and the peace of God ruling in your heart, it is doubtful you will experience much peace in your relationships with others.

16. (a) Is peace with others an option or a command? _____ (b) Why does it matter how we get along with other people? Read Mark 9:50; Romans 12:18; 1 Thessalonians 5:13.

> *"Peace is something we attain on purpose. It does not occur accidentally. Thus there is wisdom in the command: 'Seek peace, and pursue it' (Psalm 34:14)."*[5]

17. (a) Are you at odds with someone in your life? _____
    (b) What can you do to make peace with this person? Read Matthew 5:22–24.

> *"The Bible teaches us that God's peace must not only pass all understanding but all misunderstanding. People who growl and bark at each other deserve to live a dog's life."*[6]

18. Do you agree with this statement: "I think the one thing that disturbs personal relationships more than anything else is selfishness"? Why or why not? Read Philippians 2:3 and 4.

Common sense tells us that a submissive spirit is more sensible than unmovable stubbornness.

"The story is told of two mountain goats who approached one another on a narrow ledge. Realizing that there was no room to pass, they reared and bucked, but neither budged. They backed up, charged, and locked horns again, but each held his ground. Again they parted and charged; then like the Rock of Gibraltar they stood unmoveable. Finally the sensible one knelt down, and let the other one climb over him. Then they both went merrily on their way. Sometimes we too must let people walk over us."[7]

---

19. Amy Carmichael said, "In acceptance lieth peace." What does that statement mean to you?

 From My Heart

Everyone wants peace, but so few people know where to find it. Even Christians are desperately searching for peace. When you walk into a Christian bookstore or browse a Christian magazine, you notice many best-sellers are books on how to handle stress, anxiety, and the various pressures of life. Christians are spending thousands of dollars on books that tell them how to find peace. Yet they are neglecting the one Book that has been around for centuries, the Book that promises perfect peace—the Bible.

I am so glad I learned many years ago how to have peace in the midst of the storm. I learned I can have perfect peace if I keep my mind on Christ and His precious promises, if I trust Christ to do for me what I can't do for myself. Let me remind you again of the promise in Isaiah 26:3: "Thou wilt keep him in perfect peace, whose mind is stayed on thee: because he trusteth in thee." The key to this verse is trust. It will not do me much good to keep my mind on Christ and His Word if I don't really believe He can do the impossible.

"Lord, I believe; help my unbelief."

From Your Heart

Do you have peace with God, the peace of God, and peace with others?

In what area of your life are you lacking peace? What steps do you need to take to have God's perfect peace in your life?

Notes:

1. Charles H. Brent, quoted by Tileston, p. 62.

2. Mrs. Charles E. Cowman, *Streams in the Desert—1* (Grand Rapids: Zondervan Publishing House, 1965), p. 115.

3. Max Lucado, *The Applause of Heaven* (Dallas: Word Publishing, 1990), pp. 78, 79.

4. Darlow Sargeant, quoted by Cowman, pp. 310, 311.

5. Brownlow, p. 41.

6. Robert C. Gage, *Cultivating Spiritual Fruit* (Schaumburg, IL: Regular Baptist Press, 1986), p. 71.

7. Sweeting, p. 55.

LESSON 7

Long-suffering—Going on with a Knife in Your Heart

"Walk worthy of the vocation wherewith ye are called, With all lowliness and meekness, with longsuffering, forbearing one another in love" (Ephesians 4:1, 2).

When I begin to love others the way Christ loves me, I will begin to understand unconditional love. This unconditional love will *allow me to tolerate people and circumstances I once could not handle. I will truly understand what long-suffering is.*

Long-suffering is a word we seldom use, and, unfortunately, an experience some Christians never master. The word we most commonly use today for long-suffering is patience. Someone said, "Patience is not criticizing and irritating when you're being criticized and irritated; it is tolerating nagging people; it is sitting still and waiting your turn; it is the ability to keep going when you want to quit."

In this lesson we will learn how we can profit from being long-suffering with others and also with God.

1. What pictures come to your mind when you see the word "long-suffering" or "patience"?

2. (a) What grade did you give yourself in lesson 4 for "love suffereth long" (p. 39)? _____

   (b) Has your grade gone up or down since that study?

3. If love, joy, and peace are filling our lives, how will this fruit affect our patience with others?

4. Patience is a fruit of the Spirit, but what causes it to develop and grow stronger in our lives? Read James 1:2 and 3.

> *"Patience is more than endurance. A saint's life is in the hands of God like a bow and arrow in the hands of an archer. God is aiming at something the saint cannot see, and He stretches and strains, and every now and again the saint says—'I cannot stand any more.' God does not heed, He goes on stretching till His purpose is in sight, then He lets fly. Trust yourself in God's hands. For what have you need of patience just now? Maintain your relationship to Jesus Christ by the patience of faith. 'Though He slay me, yet will I wait for Him.'"[1]*

Patience with God

5. (a) Name a man in the Bible who endured more trials than most other men. _____ (b) For what is he remembered? Read James 5:11.

6. Why do we have such a hard time being patient with God when we are going through trials?

7. God took everything Job had, but Job was patient with God. What was Job's attitude?
Job 1:21

Job 2:10

8. Describe the change in Job's attitude from Job 2:10 to Job 3:1–3 and 11.

"Did Job learn patience among his flocks or with his camels or with his children when they were feasting? No, he learned it when he sat among the ashes, and scraped himself with a potsherd, and his heart was heavy because of the death of his children. Patience is a pearl which is found only in the deep seas of affliction, and only grace can find it there, bring it to the surface, and adorn the neck of faith with it."[2]

---

9. When our prayers go unanswered, our confidence may weaken and we may begin to demand answers from God. What did Job ask God? Read Job 10:1 and 2.

10. God is silent throughout the book of Job until chapter 38. When God asks us to suffer long but is also silent for a long period of time, what are we prone to think?

11. Most of us have probably experienced a dark time in our lives when we couldn't see God's hand at work, when it seemed as if He had forsaken us. If you have experienced this, would you express in words how you felt?

"There is no patience so hard as that which endures, 'as seeing Him who is invisible'; it is the waiting for hope."[3]

---

12. (a) Did God ever explain to Job why his trial had occurred? Read Job 38—41.

(b) What rebuke did God give Job in 40:1 and 2?

13. What did Job's long-suffering teach him? Read Job 42:1–6.

> *"Extraordinary afflictions are not always the punishment of extraordinary sins, but sometimes the trial of extraordinary graces. God hath many sharp-cutting instruments, and rough files for the polishing of His jewels; and those He especially loves, and means to make the most resplendent, He hath oftenest His tools upon."*[4]

14. How would you grade yourself on your patience with God?

Patience with others

15. In what kinds of situations do you or some of your friends live that call for great patience?

16. When you think you have too many trials, what will help change your perspective?

> *"If you will follow Me, I will cause every reversal to count as rehearsal for even greater victories than were previously planned."*[5]

17. How does our patience affect those who intentionally hurt us? Read Romans 12:20.

18. What does Joseph's experience teach us about committing our circumstances to God and then patiently waiting to see what God will do? Read Genesis 50:20.

"If Joseph had not been Egypt's prisoner, he never would have been Egypt's governor. The iron chain about his feet ushered in the golden chain about his neck."[6]

---

19. Ephesians 4:2 and 3 tell us to be patient and forbearing with one another. How can you continue to be patient with a person who continually fails to live up to his or her word and your expectations? Read 1 Peter 4:8.

If you have learned to walk
A little more sure-footedly than I,
Be patient with my stumbling then
And know that only as I do my best and try
May I attain the goal
For which we both are striving.

If through experience, your soul
Has gained heights which I
As yet in dim-lit vision see,
Hold out your hand and point the way,
Lest from its straightness I should stray,
And walk a mile with me.[7]

20. Instead of letting another's actions irritate us, how should we view the situation? Read Colossians 3:13.

21. When we get tired of waiting for God to change a person or situation, what are we—like Abraham and Sarah of old—prone to do? Read Genesis 16:1 and 2.

22. (a) Who is the most difficult person in your life, the person with whom you need to be most patient? Write the person's initials here. _____ (b) What are you expecting from this person?

   (c) Did God say you could expect that?

   "My soul, wait thou only upon God; for my expectation is from him" (Psalm 62:5).

 From My Heart

   I once read that patience is accepting a difficulty without giving God a deadline to remove it. I want patience; I need patience. However, I do not like the process by which it is usually developed in my life. It is usually a slow process, and I want it now. I can relate to the bumper sticker that says, "Lord, give me patience—and give it to me now!" Being patient and learning to wait is hard in this hurry-up, rush-rush society.

   Sometime ago God sent an interruption into my life that I had a hard time accepting. I began to experience constant fatigue and had to drop out of activities I really enjoyed. First I stopped playing tennis; then I had to stop teaching my ladies' Bible class. I kept saying, "Lord, why are You doing this to me?" In His Word I found these answers: "Slow down; I want you to *see* and *know* some new things!"

Stand still, and *see*—Exodus 14:13

Be still, and *know*—Psalm 46:10

I now *see* that God doesn't have to give me answers; He just wants me to *know* that while I am waiting, I can trust Him.

> In every life
> There's a pause that is better than onward rush,
> Better than hewing or mightiest doing;
> 'Tis the standing still at Sovereign will.
>
> There's a hush that is better than ardent speech,
> Better than sighing or wilderness crying;
> 'Tis the being still at Sovereign will.
>
> The pause and the hush sing a double song
> In unison low and for all time long.
> O human soul, God's working plan
> Goes on, nor needs the aid of man!
> > Stand still, and see!
> > Be still, and know![8]

From Your Heart

Have you gotten so low you've given up on God and decided He isn't going to help you? What did you learn from this lesson that can renew your faith and trust in God? Write down the initials of three people with whom you need to be more patient.

Notes:

1. Chambers, p. 129.

2. Tom Carter, compiler, *Spurgeon at His Best* (Grand Rapids: Baker Book House, 1988), p. 357.

3. George Matheson, quoted by Cowman, p. 235.

4. Archbishop Leighton, quoted by Cowman, p. 124.

5. Charles Slagle, *From the Father's Heart* (Shippensburg, PA: Destiny Image Publishers, 1989), p. 61.

6. Cowman, p. 281.

7. Jo Petty, compiler, *Apples of Gold* (Norwalk, CT: The C. R. Gibson Co., 1962), p. 42.

8. V. Raymond Edman, *The Disciplines of Life* (Wheaton, IL: Scripture Press, 1948), p. 83.

LESSON 8

Gentleness—Being Kind, Tenderhearted, and Forgiving

"And be ye kind one to another, tenderhearted, forgiving one another, even as God for Christ's sake hath forgiven you"
(Ephesians 4:32).

When I begin to love others the way Christ loves me, I will begin to understand unconditional love. This unconditional love will *change me. I will not only be able to tolerate people I couldn't handle before, but I will also find myself being kind and gentle with them.*

The word translated "gentleness" in Galatians 5:22 can be translated "kindness." Gentleness is kind, and kindness is gentle. We will use both words in this lesson.

1. Write your definition of gentleness, or kindness.

> *". . . 'Keep tough and tender'—tough on ourselves and tender with others. That is the spirit of gentleness."[1]*

2. When you think of the words "kindness" and "gentleness," what friend, national figure, or Bible character comes to your mind?

3. What are the similarities between kindness and mercy?

4. How does Luke 6:31 relate to showing kindness to others?

"Gentleness is illustrated by the way we would handle a carton of exquisite crystal glasses; it is the recognition that the human personality is valuable but fragile, and must be handled with care."[2]

---

5. What else is involved in kindness? Read Ephesians 4:32.

"Be kind. Remember that everyone you meet is fighting a hard battle."[3]

---

6. Read Matthew 5:43–48. How are a believer and unbeliever alike according to verses 46 and 47?

7. When we live a Spirit-controlled life, how will we show kindness in a supernatural way? Read Matthew 5:43 and 44 and 1 Peter 2:20.

". . . Kindness should be of such a quality that we can even love our enemies, bless those who curse us, do good to those that hate us, pray for those who despise and persecute us. . . . To live this way calls for courage. It means that some of those to whom we extend kindness will turn around and kick us in the teeth. It means that we will often be snubbed or scorned, and that our best intentions will sometimes be misunderstood and misconstrued."[4]

---

8. According to Matthew 18:21 and 22, how many times should we forgive a person?

9. Henry Ward Beecher said, "Though the world needs reproof and . . . correction, it needs kindness more." What kind of spirit must we develop to keep showing kindness when we know some people may show no appreciation for it? Read 2 Timothy 2:24.

10. When we love our enemies, they will probably not love us in return. When we are kind to our friends, they may stab us in the back. How does Galatians 6:7 encourage us to keep sowing love and kindness?

"God has a secret method by which he recompenses his saints: he sees to it that they become the prime beneficiaries of their own benefactions!"[5]

---

11. How does Jesus look upon our kindness to others? Read Matthew 25:35–40.

12. Kindness speaks peace, lifts loads, inspires the down-hearted. It is often done in secret and seen only by God. Many people are too busy to be kind. What are some ways we could show kindness to others if we would take the time?

13. Read Matthew 11:28 and 29. How do these verses describe Christ?

"Meek and lowly" in these verses could be translated "gentle and humble." Here is another interesting insight into this phrase: "The Syriac New Testament translates the word *gentle* as 'restful'; accordingly Jesus' expression is, 'Come to me . . . and I will *rest* you . . . for I am *restful* . . . and you shall find *rest* for yourselves.' Christ's whole demeanor was such that people were often restful in his presence."[6]

14. If we are gentle, kind, and Christlike, how will this affect the people around us?

15. Do you put people at ease when they are around you? Evaluate your attitudes and actions. Why do you think people would or would not feel at ease around you?

16. Do you picture yourself as gentle and kind with others? If your answer is no, here are two things to do to help develop a gentle spirit.

    • Decide if you want to be gentle and kind in your dealings with others or if you want to keep your spirit of "Hey, that's just me; I say what I feel."

    • Ask these questions of a person who will be honest with you: Am I blunt and abrupt with people? Am I dogmatic and intimidating?

> *"If you cannot win by being a gentle lady or a kind gentleman, then the winning is not worth your stooping beneath yourself which would be no victory at all. This is the more excellent and kingly way: 'And the servant of the Lord must not strive; but be gentle unto all men . . . patient.'—II Timothy 2:24."*[7]

17. "But we were gentle among you, even as a nurse cherisheth her children" (1 Thessalonians 2:7). How does a loving mother care for her children?

18. How can we exemplify a mother's gentleness in dealing
    with others?

Someone once said, "Gentleness is stooping down to
encourage another." I think the following story, told by Jerry
Jenkins, is a beautiful picture of gentleness—a caring heart.

"A couple of years ago I was at a convention waiting to
chat with Roosevelt Grier, the massive former pro football
player, now a minister. Just before I got to him, a woman
brought her young teen son, who clearly had Down's syn-
drome, for a handshake and an autograph from Rosey.

The big man could have simply smiled, shaken hands,
and signed. But he did more. He dropped to one knee,
putting him at eye level with the boy. Rosey put his arm
around him, pulled him close, and spoke to him quietly. I
couldn't help myself. I edged closer.

'Are you a Christian?' Rosey asked.

'Yes, sir.'

'Praise the Lord. Can I pray with you?'

The boy was overcome. All he could do was nod. As
they prayed, the mother wept. When she tried to thank
Rosey, he simply winked at her. Then, to the boy, he said,
'You take care of your mama now, you hear?'

'Yes, sir.'

Oh that we might all be caught being kinder than kind."[8]

 From My Heart

As I was writing this lesson the following song kept
popping into my mind:

> Show a little bit of love and kindness,
> Never go along with hatred's blindness
> Take a little time to reach for joy,
> And wear a happy face;
> Sing a little bit when the days are dreary,
> Give a little help to a friend who's weary—
> That's the way to make the world a happy place![9]

Wouldn't it be great if we all showed just a little extra love and kindness each day? God has given us all gifts and talents, but one gift we all can have is kindness. However, I have found this gift is valuable only when I give it away. I will never be too old to be kind; and sorrow, fatigue, and weakness do not excuse me from passing on the gift of kindness. Remember that Jesus said, "Inasmuch as ye have done it [showed kindness] unto one of the least of these my brethren, ye have done it unto me" (Matthew 25:40).

"Lord, help me to show a little extra love and kindness each day!"

From Your Heart

Do you have the same picture of gentleness and kindness as you did when you started the lesson? What did you think before you studied the lesson? What do you think now?

Notes:

1. Jerry Bridges, *The Practice of Godliness* (Colorado Springs, CO: NavPress, 1983), p. 227.

2. Bridges, p. 220.

3. Harry Thompson, quoted by Blanchard, p. 178.

4. W. Phillip Keller, *A Gardener Looks at the Fruits of the Spirit* (Waco, TX: Word Books, 1979), pp. 130, 131.

5. I. D. E. Thomas, quoted by Blanchard, p. 178.

6. William Hendriksen, quoted by Bridges, p. 222.

7. Brownlow, p. 51.

8. Jerry B. Jenkins, "For Starters," *Moody* (June 1991), p. 6.

9. John W. Peterson, "Show a Little Bit of Love and Kindness," *Sing 'N' Praise Hymnal* (Dallas: The Zondervan Corp., 1976), No. 117.

LESSON 9

Goodness—Do You Like the Idea of Being a Servant?

"Ye shall know them by their fruits. . . . Even so every good tree bringeth forth good fruit; but a corrupt tree bringeth forth evil fruit" (Matthew 7:16, 17).

When I begin to love others the way Christ loves me, I will begin to understand unconditional love. This unconditional love will *change me. I will not only be able to tolerate people I once couldn't handle, but I will even find myself being good to them.*

A healthy fruit tree will bear good fruit. A Spirit-controlled believer will bear good fruit. "The fruit of the Spirit is love, joy, peace, longsuffering, gentleness, goodness . . ." (Galatians 5:22). One of the most accurate tests of a good person is the fruit she bears.

1. Kindness and goodness are closely related; sometimes it is hard to distinguish between them. (a) How did you define kindness in lesson 8?

   (b) How would you define goodness?

2. How does Acts 10:38 describe the actions of the Lord Jesus?

3. When we were "created in Christ Jesus" (saved), what purpose did God have in mind for our lives? Read Ephesians 2:8–10.

"Tis God gives skill,
But not without men's hands; He
could not make
Antonio Stradivari's violins
Without Antonio. "[1]

4. Read Ephesians 2:10 again. What does "walk in them" imply about doing good works?

"I'm going your way, so let us go hand in hand. You help me and I'll help you. We shall not be here very long, for soon death, the kind old nurse, will come back and rock us all to sleep. Let us help one another while we may. "[2]

5. In 1 Timothy 5:10 Paul described the widows as being "well reported of for good works." What things did Paul enumerate that were part of a widow's daily living?

6. How does this list relate to housewives who feel they would like a more glamorous place to do their good works?

7. Stay-at-home ladies sometimes feel a bit envious of single women and career women, feeling their lives are more exciting. If you are a stay-at-home wife and mother, do you see this position as an opportunity to do the good works "God hath before ordained that [you] should walk in them"? Why do you feel this way?

I thought some of you young mothers might enjoy the following anecdote:

"Some local folks received a letter from friends who lived in another city. In it the happy couple announced the birth of their fourth child. As a gift the local couple sent the new parents a playpen.

Two weeks later the new mother responded with this note: 'Thanks, many thanks, and thanks again for the playpen. It comes in so handy. I sit in it every afternoon and read and think. In it the children can't get near me.'"[3]

8. If you have not viewed your job as housewife as a valuable vocation, what needs to change in order for you to start thinking this way?

9. Galatians 6:10 tells us we are to be especially mindful of fellow believers when we are doing good to others. Some women get so involved in helping others that they forget their first responsibility. Whom are we to care for first? Read 1 Timothy 5:8.

10. For whom else are we to care? Whom does "all men" in Galatians 6:10 include?

"It is one thing to do good in a few, or even in a number of, isolated instances; it is quite another to face cheerfully the prospect of doing some particular deed of goodness day in and day out for an interminable period of time, particularly if those deeds are taken for granted by the recipients. But true goodness does not look to the recipients, nor even to the results, of its deeds for its reward. It looks to God alone, and, finding his smile of approval, it gains the needed strength to carry on."[4]

---

11. If someone called you a "Dorcas," what would that say about you? Read Acts 9:36.

12. Sometimes it costs us to do good. What might the world call you instead of a "Dorcas"?

13. Goodness lifts loads and helps the helpless. It is often done in secret and seen only by God. Many people are too busy to help others. Review the things you listed as acts of kindness in lesson 8, question 12 (page 69). What good deeds could you add to the list?

"Accept the cost of good deeds in time, thought, and effort. But remember that opportunities for doing good are not interruptions in God's plan for us, but part of that plan. We always have time to do what God wants us to do."[5]

---

14. The child of God has no excuse for not doing good works. What help is available to us according to 2 Corinthians 9:8?

> Through this toilsome world, alas!
> Once and only once I pass;
> If a kindness I may show,
> If a good deed I may do
> To a suffering fellow man,
> Let me do it while I can.
> No delay, for it is plain
> I shall not pass this way again.[6]

15. How can we be eyes, ears, hands, feet, and a strong back to a world in need?

Eyes

Ears

Hands

Feet

Strong back

> Lord, make me an instrument of your peace!
> Where there is hatred, let me sow love;
> Where there is injury, pardon;
> Where there is doubt, faith;
> Where there is despair, hope;
> Where there is darkness, light;
> Where there is sadness, joy.
> O Divine Master, grant that I may not so much seek
> To be consoled, as to console;
> To be understood, as to understand;
> To be loved, as to love.
> For it is in giving that we receive;
> It is in pardoning that we are pardoned;
> It is in dying that we are born to eternal life.[7]

16. (a) Would you classify yourself as a selfish or a giving person according to Philippians 2:3? _____
(b) How does this verse say we should see ourselves in relation to others?

_____

"Although . . . disciples are to be seen doing good works, they must not do good works in order to be seen."[8]

_____

17. Read John 13:14–17. Why did Christ wash the disciples' feet?

18. Do you like the idea of being called a servant?

19. When a person serves day after day with a self-sacrificing spirit and receives no thanks or reward for it, how do we know this service does not go unnoticed by the Lord? Read Matthew 25:21.

Goodness is an investment you can be sure will never fail!

 From My Heart

As I was writing this lesson, I was reminded of three young ladies who were discussing marriage. One young lady said, "When I grow up, I want to marry a doctor so I can be sick for nothing." The next gal said, "When I grow up, I want to marry a lawyer so I can be bad for nothing." The last young lady said, "When I grow up, I want to marry a preacher so I can be good for nothing."

Do you ever feel as if you've been good and your goodness has counted as nothing? Maybe you live with an unloving spouse who never notices your goodness or speaks a kind word to you. Maybe you have reared children who accepted your goodness but gave nothing back in return, not even a thank you for all the sacrifice you made for them.

Ladies, I applaud you. Your good deeds do not go unnoticed by Christ. One day you will hear Him say, "Well done, thou good and faithful servant" (Matthew 25:21). I have a feeling that verse is what keeps many of you going when you want to quit.

"Lord, help me also to remember this truth when I feel like sitting on the sidelines instead of staying in the race."

From Your Heart

We are not saved by our good works, but we are saved to do good works. What good works are you involved in that demonstrate to others that you are a child of God? Do any of your attitudes or actions need to change after studying this lesson? If so, what?

Notes:

1. George Eliot, quoted in *Moody Alumni* (Spring 1992).

2. William Morris, quoted by Lillian Eichler Watson, editor, *Light from Many Lamps* (New York: Simon and Schuster, 1951), p. 198.

3. Quoted from *Parables, Etc.* (Platteville, CO: Saratoga Press, September 1991).

4. Bridges, p. 241.

5. Bridges, p. 243.

6. Gail Harvey, editor, *Poems of Inspiration and Comfort* (New York: Avenel Books, 1990), p. 12.

7. Francis of Assisi.

8. Paul B. Levertoff, quoted by Blanchard, p. 126.

LESSON 10

Faithfulness—You Can Depend on Me!

*"Moreover it is required in stewards,
that a man be found faithful" (1 Corinthians 4:2).*

When I begin to love others the way Christ loves me, I will begin to understand unconditional love. This unconditional love will *develop a faithfulness in me that will enable me to do things I once said I could never do.*

"Faithfulness" is an accurate translation of the Greek word for "faith" in Galatians 5:22. If you have never studied the fruit of the Spirit before, you may have assumed (as I did) that the word "faith" meant trusting or believing. However, in this context, the accurate translation is "faithfulness." This faithfulness denotes fidelity, a faithful devotion to our obligations, duty, or vows, especially in relation to other people. Synonyms for faithful are dependable, reliable, trustworthy, and loyal.

In lesson 9 we learned that goodness was reaching out to others and caring for them, even to those who don't deserve it. This goodness is not a wishy-washy, when-I-feel-like-it action. It is steady and continual; it is faithful. We will look at three aspects of faithfulness: The Father's Faithfulness, The Son's Faithfulness, and Our Faithfulness.

The Father's Faithfulness

1. To see the caliber of faithfulness expected of us, we cannot look to men and women as examples. Who alone is a constant example of faithfulness? Read Psalm 36:5–9.

2. We live in an insecure, unsteady world. How does Psalm 119:90 assure you of God's faithfulness and give you a sense of security?

80

3. We also live in a generation of truce-breakers. People take vows, make pledges, make promises, and then break them with hardly a twinge of guilt. What promise has God made to His children? Read Deuteronomy 7:9.

"The Lord will go through with His covenant engagements. Whatever He takes in hand He will accomplish; hence past mercies are guarantees for the future and admirable reasons for continuing to cry unto Him."[1]

---

4. According to Psalm 143:1, what is one area in which God is faithful?

The Son's Faithfulness

God the Father sent His Son, Jesus Christ, to this earth to be a servant and to die for the sins of all men (Matthew 20:28). Let's look at Christ's faithfulness to us in finishing the job He came to do.

5. Why was it necessary for Christ to be a servant as well as our Savior? Read Matthew 20:26–28.

6. (a) Ponder this question: Was Christ's faithfulness to us ever tested? _____ (b) How? Read Isaiah 50:6 and 7 and Matthew 26:51–56.

7. How do Christ's last words in John 19:30 demonstrate His faithfulness to His God-appointed mission?

Our Faithfulness

8. How should the example of Christ challenge us in the area of faithfulness?

9. Do you always finish what you start? Why or why not?

"When I was in the sixth grade, one of our penmanship exercises was this verse, which has rung in my mind ever since:

If a task is once begun
Never leave it till it's done.
Be the labor great or small,
Do it well or not at all.

We will finish our course with joy if we stick to the assignment. We will be able to say as Jesus did, 'I have finished the work You gave me.' "[2]

---

10. What are some words that are the opposite of faithfulness?

11. If you were asked to describe yourself, which of these descriptions would be appropriate? Circle one.

    Faithful and dependable—I'm always there; I finish what I start; I try to do my part; I keep my word.

    Unfaithful and undependable—I'm there when I feel like it; I lose interest and drop out; I often forget what I said I would do; I don't always do what I said I would.

12. When you think of a faithful person, who comes to your mind?

13. The Bible has some special promises for the faithful person. What are two of them, according to the following verses?
Proverbs 28:20

Matthew 25:21

14. To whom do we need to be faithful and loyal?

"Once I have promised, dear Lord, help me 'deliver the goods.' A broken promise is awfully hard to mend and so are broken hearts. . . . Besides my family needs to know there is someone in this whole wide disillusioning world they can always depend on. Thank you, Lord, that you are always dependable, even when I'm not."[3]

---

15. How does a believer display her faithfulness to Christ?
Hebrews 10:25

Psalm 100:2

Psalm 119:16

Christ has no hands but our hands
To do His work today;
He has no feet but our feet
To lead men in His way;
He has no tongue but our tongue
To tell men how He died;
He has no help but our help
To bring them to His side.[4]

16. (a) Write your description of a faithful and loyal friend.

    (b) How does Proverbs 17:17 picture this friend?

17. A loyal friend will stick with you. What else will she do according to Proverbs 27:6?

"He who ceases to be your friend never was a good one."[5]

---

18. You could risk a friendship by "speaking the truth in love" as we are told to do in Ephesians 4:15. What are some questions you might ask yourself before you confront your friend?

19. How can some married couples so easily forget the vow they took, "until death we do part"?

"Committed!
No turning back.
No way out.
The very thought sends chills up the spines of
so many whose lives thrive on non-commitment.
Whether in a marriage, a mortgage, or a move, they

fear that ultimate prison of never turning back....
The fear of commitment is epidemic in the
Western world. Students wait longer and longer to
make a choice of major. Couples enter marriage
tentatively with an easy escape clause. Men and
women take jobs with a wary reserve that keeps
them looking for something better....
What is the root?
Selfishness."[6]

20. When we take the attitude, "I deserve to be happy; I
don't have to take this," what have we forgotten? Read
Matthew 5:10–12 and John 15:20.

21. Read 1 Peter 1:15 and 16. Christ didn't call us to be
happy but to be _____.

God wants us to be holy, different people. He wants us
to reflect Christ in this dark, sinful world. Our faithfulness to
Christ and to others will cause us to shine as bright lights in
this dark world.

 From My Heart

I have made two verbal life commitments, one to the
Lord and one to my husband. I have learned my first commitment must be to God. I made this commitment many years
ago as I knelt beside a chair in my dining room and told the
Lord He could have my life. I had no idea how God could ever
make a pastor's wife out of me. But I told him I would faithfully stand by my husband's side and do the best I could.

I have come to realize through the years that, the more
I love the Lord and am faithful to Him, the more I know how
to love my husband and faithfully stand with him through
thick and thin. I have never forgotten the following poem
that I read many years ago:

My soul will never, never be yours alone; . . .
There is a love that worships God alone as King!
There is a love that unto Him alone I bring;
If you refuse Him what is His by right
How could I love thee as I might?
But bid me live for Him, then know
That I would die for thee!
Loving Him best I shall love thee the more;
And my lips will always seek your own,
But my soul can never, never be yours alone.[7]

Love and faithfulness to a mate are a great heritage to pass on to your children. I have three married sons, and I made this counted cross-stitch plaque for each son: "The greatest gift a father can give his children is to love their mother."

Remember, there is no ability like dependability. God counts faithfulness as a great thing. He does not tell us many things He will say to us when we see Him face to face. He does say some of His children will hear, "Well done, good and *faithful* servant."

I want to hear that declaration; do you?

From Your Heart

Does the word "commitment" scare you? Why or why not? Have you ever committed your life to someone or something and promised to be faithful? To whom or what? Do you review your commitments from time to time to see if you are being faithful to them?

Notes:
1. C. H. Spurgeon, quoted by Cowman, p. 166.
2. Elisabeth Elliot, *Discipline: The Glad Surrender* (Old Tappan, NJ: Fleming H. Revell Co., 1982), p. 137.
3. Phyllis C. Michael, *Is My Head on Straight?* (Waco, TX: Word Books, 1976), p. 42.
4. Annie Johnson Flint, quoted by Al Bryant, compiler, *Favorite Poems* (Grand Rapids: Zondervan Publishing House, 1957), p. 13.
5. Benjamin R. De Jong, *Uncle Ben's Quotebook* (Irvine, CA: Harvest House Publishers, 1976), p. 163.
6. Jerry White, *The Power of Commitment* (Colorado Springs, CO: NavPress, 1985), pp. 13, 14.
7. Louis H. Evans, *Your Marriage—Duel or Duet?* (Westwood, NJ: Fleming H. Revell Co., 1962), p. 90.

LESSON 11

Meekness—Humility That Allows Me to Submit

"Take my yoke upon you, and learn of me; for I am meek and lowly in heart" (Matthew 11:29).

When I begin to love others the way Christ loves me, I will begin to understand unconditional love. This unconditional love will *be demonstrated by a humble, submissive spirit. This submissive spirit is more interested in serving than being served.*

If you were to ask the man on the street to define meekness, he would probably answer, "weakness, mousy, or timid." But meekness is not weakness; on the contrary, it is power under control.

"Humility" could be substituted for the word "meekness," but this is an active humility, communicated by doing something. How does humility express itself? It is kind, gentle, not easily provoked, has no lingering malice, never seeks earthly recognition, and always thinks of others rather than self. Christ Himself is the perfect example. He said, "Learn of me; for I am meek and lowly in heart" (Matthew 11:29).

In this lesson we will see how to be meek, or humble, in our relationship to God, to ourselves, and to others.

1. How would you illustrate meekness?

2. Why is meekness not weakness?

Humility in our relationship to God

3. A meek person is one with a humble, submissive spirit toward God. How does the example of Christ help us in this regard? Read Luke 22:42.

4. When our circumstances are difficult and people are abusing us, how can we humbly accept this difficulty as from a kind and loving Heavenly Father? Read Psalm 18:30.

"The meek are those who quietly submit themselves before God, to His Word, to His rod, and who follow His directions and comply to His designs and are gentle toward all men."[1]

---

5. We mentioned the palms-up life in lesson 5 (page 48). What is the palms-up life?

Living the Palms-up Life

P lace your palms up before God.
A llow God to take what He wants.
L et God be free to give what He wants.
M entally picture yourself turning loose of everything.
S ay to God, "Give what You want, and take what You want."

U ntil you learn to trust God totally, you will be uptight, living with clenched fists.
P alms-up living is relaxed living—turning loose, opening up, and trusting God completely.

> One by one He took them from me,
> All the things I valued most,
> Until I was empty handed
> Every glittering toy was lost.

And I walked earth's highways, grieving
In my rags and poverty,
Till I heard His voice inviting,
"Lift your empty hands to Me!"

So I held my hands toward Heaven,
And He filled them with a store
Of His own transcendent riches,
Till my hands could hold no more.

And at last I comprehended
With my stupid mind and dull,
That God could not pour His riches
Into hands already full.[2]

Humility in relationship to ourselves

6. When a person is truly humble before God, how will she express this humility regarding her gifts, attainments, and abilities? Read 1 Corinthians 4:7.

"Isn't it marvelous and encouraging that meek peo-ple without trying receive more appreciation and acclaim than the swaggering swell heads who try so hard for a place in the world? So if you want esteem and goodwill, be mild rather than proud, and be mild rather than brutish."[3]

---

7. James 1:21 says we need to receive God's Word with meekness. Why do we need humility when considering God's Word and its application to our lives?

8. Why does a proud person find it hard to submit to the will of another?

9. Following the example of Christ as described in Philippians 2:5–7, what kind of spirit does a humble person display?

10. Read Matthew 20:26–28. What is involved in having a servant's spirit?

". . . A lady had been for years rebelling fearfully against a little act of service which she knew was right, but which she hated. I saw her, out of the depths of despair, and without any feeling whatever, give her will in that matter up into the hands of her Lord, and begin to say to Him, 'Thy will be done; Thy will be done!' *And in one short hour that very thing began to look sweet and precious to her."[4]*

Humility in our relationship to others

11. Why do we need humility when confronting someone who needs correction? Read Galatians 6:1.

12. Second Timothy 2:24–26 says we need humility in dealing with those who oppose us. Why is this?

13. How do we need to view people before we can begin to show a spirit of humility and submission? Read Philippians 2:3.

"In life we learn either humility or humiliation. If we allow pride to control our lives, the Lord will humble us. That is humiliation. If we put Christ in full charge of our lives, He will receive the glory. That is humility. The choice is ours."[5]

---

14. To whom do you have the hardest time submitting?

15. Read Ephesians 5:18–22. Why do so many women have a problem with verse 22?

> *"How soon marriage counseling sessions would end if husbands and wives were competing in thoughtful self-denial!"*[6]

16. Submission does not mean a woman is owned or operated by her husband. What does it mean? Read Ephesians 5:22–24.

17. What is the role and purpose of a wife?

> *"One plus one equals one may not be an accurate mathematical concept, but it is an accurate description of God's intention for the marriage relationship."*[7]

18. Being submissive does not mean being inferior. The Father is the Head of Christ; the husband is the head of the wife. They are equal and one, but one is in charge.
    (a) Read John 10:30. To Whom was Christ equal?_____

    (b) Read Luke 22:42. To Whom did Christ submit? _____

    (c) Read Ephesians 5:31. To whom is the wife equal?

    _____

    (d) Read Ephesians 5:22. To whom is the wife to be

    submissive?_____

Christ was equal to the Father, yet in submission to the Father. Likewise, the wife is equal to the husband, yet in submission to the husband.

> *"If you do not recognize that God designed you and your husband to complement each other, you may try to force your husband to act and respond to life as you do. Should you succeed, he would have to switch to the feminine role of being the responder, abandoning his masculine responsibilities. If you recognize, however, that by nature your roles are different, you can develop your feminine traits and become a truly feminine woman."[8]*

19. Jesus was in total submission to the Father and gave up every right He had, but He did not lose His identity. How do we know this? Read John 17:1–4.

20. (a) Did Christ think the Father was unfair because He chose Christ to be a servant? _____
    (b) What was Christ's attitude according to Philippians 2:8?

21. How does Christ's example relate to us in this area of submission to God, to our husbands, and to others?

 *From My Heart*

May I remind you again that meekness is not weakness. Meekness is power under control, the strength to humble yourself and submit when everything in you wants to resist. A meek person has learned to submit to the will of her Lord and Master, Jesus Christ, and to others.

Do you view submission as a glad surrender or a curse? I'm glad I can finally view submission as a glad surrender.

This did not happen quickly, but slowly I began to view submission as a blessing rather than a curse. When I finally wanted to do God's will as much as I had wanted my own will, I began to understand why Jesus said, "Blessed are the meek: for they shall inherit the earth" (Matthew 5:5). The meek do not struggle or contend with God but accept whatever He chooses for their life on this earth. Therefore they are satisfied and content with the Father's plans and appointments for them.

Back in the early 1800s Hannah Whitall Smith wrote these words, which still apply to us today:

> *"It is wonderful what miracles God works in wills that are utterly surrendered to Him. He turns hard things into easy, and bitter things into sweet. It is not that He puts easy things in the place of the hard, but He actually changes the hard thing into an easy one, and makes us love to do the thing we before so hated. While we rebel against the yoke, and try to avoid it, we find it hard and galling. But when we 'take the yoke upon us' with a consenting will, we find it easy and comfortable."*[9]

"Lord, I do want to know more about You so I might learn to be 'meek and lowly in heart' as You were."

From Your Heart

If you had to write in one sentence what you learned from this lesson, what would you write? What changes do you need to make in your life in regard to submission? Are you willing to change? What is the first thing you are going to do?

Notes:
1. Matthew Henry.
2. Martha Snell Nicholson.
3. Brownlow, p. 89.
4. Smith, p. 189.
5. Gage, pp. 115, 116.
6. Walter J. Chantry, quoted by Blanchard, p. 197.
7. Wayne Mack, quoted by Blanchard, p. 197.
8. Darien B. Cooper, *You Can Be the Wife of a Happy Husband* (Wheaton, IL: Victor Books, 1974), pp. 66, 67.
9. Smith, pp. 189, 190.

LESSON 12

Self-control—Learning When to Say No

"Finally, brethren, whatsoever things are true, whatsoever things are honest, whatsoever things are just, whatsoever things are pure, whatsoever things are lovely, whatsoever things are of good report; if there be any virtue, and if there be any praise, think on these things" (Philippians 4:8).

When I begin to love others the way Christ loves me, I will begin to understand unconditional love. This unconditional love *allows me to control my emotions and will. I must be Spirit-controlled, but I must also be self-controlled if I am ever to see the beautiful fruit of the Spirit bloom in my life.*

It is interesting that the fruit of the Spirit starts with love and ends with self-control. Love and self-control seem to be like two bookends holding all the other virtues in place. Without unconditional love, you cannot experience joy, peace, long-suffering, gentleness, goodness, faithfulness, and meekness in your life. From the other end, without self-control you will not walk in the Spirit long enough to see the fruit develop in your life. I picture it like this:

LOVE, joy, peace, long-suffering, gentleness, goodness, faithfulness, meekness, **SELF-CONTROL**

The word "temperance" may also be translated "self-control." It literally means "inner power or strength." It is the willpower not to act on impulse or not to indulge when you know you shouldn't. Self-control is a fruit of the Spirit, but we must cooperate with God in order for Him to accomplish His work in our lives.

1. What is your definition of self-control?

2. How does 1 Corinthians 6:12 relate to self-control?

3. How does Proverbs 25:28 picture a person who cannot control his spirit?

"He who reigns within himself, and rules passions, desires, and fears, is more than a king."[1]

---

4. What are some physical temptations to which we must learn to say no?

5. In contrast to the example of Christ in Mark 1:35, what is an important area of life in which many of us tend to be lazy?

6. The real reason for laziness in personal prayer and Bible study is lack of self-discipline. But what excuses do we commonly use?

"There is always enough time to do the will of God. *For that we can never say, 'I don't have time.' When we find ourselves frantic and frustrated, harried and harrassed and 'hassled,' it is a sign that we are running on our own schedule, not on God's. . . . 'My burden is light,' Jesus said. It is the addition of burdens God never meant us to carry that weighs us down."*[2]

---

7. (a) What do most Christians have in their homes that may cause them to have impure sexual desires?_____
(b) What is the solution to this temptation?

8. Have you ever been hooked on TV soap operas or a tabloid like the *National Inquirer?* What do these things do to your mind?

9. How can a woman gain victory or self-control in this area?

> I have to live with myself, and so,
> I want to be fit for myself to know;
> I want to be able as days go by
> Always to look myself in the eye. . . .
> I can never hide myself from me
> I see what others may never see;
> I know what others may never know:
> I can never fool myself and so
> Whatever happens, I want to be
> Self respecting, and conscience free.[3]

10. Someone has said, "Our minds are mental greenhouses." What does that statement mean to you?

11. How can Philippians 4:8 help us control our thought life?

12. In 1 Corinthians 9:24–27 Paul compared the Christian life to running a race. The same picture is given in Hebrews 12:1 and 2. According to these verses, what do we need to do to run a good race?

Walking in the Spirit is not for weak-willed, whining women controlled by their whims, but for Spirit-filled, striving servants who are controlled by the Holy Spirit.

13. Take some time for honest evaluation. Do you have weights or sins in your life that are hindering your walk with Christ and the Spirit's control in your life? What are they?

14. What do we need to do to lay aside weights and sins that control us?

15. According to Romans 6:16–18 and 2 Peter 2:19, we become slaves to whatever controls us. What controls you?

"Every freedom has a corresponding bondage, and every bondage has a corresponding freedom. You can be free from the toothbrush and a slave to cavities, or you can be a slave to the toothbrush and free from cavities.

You cannot be free from the toothbrush and free from cavities. That kind of freedom does not exist. By nature that is what we want. Absolute freedom. But we can't have it. . . . There is no such thing as total freedom. Always, there is one bondage, and one freedom. You choose."[4]

---

16. Is there an area of your life that is out of control? If you
    answer yes to one or more of the questions below,
    something is controlling you rather than your
    controlling it. Are you in control or being controlled?

    • Are you trying to hide something you are doing?
    • Are you making excuses for what you are doing by
      blaming others or circumstances for your lack of
      control in this area of your life?
    • Do you continue to do this even though you have
      repeatedly tried to stop?
    • Do you say, "I can stop whenever I want to," even
      while you continue to do it?
    • Do you cover up this area of your life by lying about it?
    • Are you continuing a habit that you know does not
      please the Lord?

    > *"No horse gets anywhere until he is harnessed.*
    > *No steam or gas ever drives anything until it is*
    > * confined.*
    > *No Niagara is ever turned into light and power until*
    > * it is tunneled.*
    > *No life ever grows great until it is*
    > * focused,*
    > * dedicated,*
    > * disciplined."[5]*

17. We cannot practice self-control and gratify selfish desires
    at the same time. What do the following passages of
    Scripture teach us regarding having victory over these
    desires in our lives? Read Galatians 5:16–18 and Romans
    7:18–22.

    > *"Common sense tells you when to say no to an extra*
    > *helping of cholesterol-laden dessert. Common sense*
    > *tells you that if your financial out-go exceeds your*
    > *financial income, your upkeep will be your downfall.*

> *But self-control is something more. It is a fruit of the Spirit . . . the product of a life empowered and directed by the Spirit's impulse.*
>
> *With His help you can be guided past the desire of the moment to the greater desire of pleasing God at all times. Question: Are you a lover of pleasure more than a lover of God? (2 Timothy 3:4)."*[6]

18. One description of the last days is that men will be "lovers of pleasures more than lovers of God" (2 Timothy 3:1, 4). What does that mean?

19. How does lack of self-control affect one's husband, children, or relatives?

20. In what area of your life do you most need to exercise self-control?

> *"Commitment without discipline is like a luxurious car without gasoline: it looks great, but it's going nowhere. Sincere and earnest commitments are useless without the discipline to carry them out.*
>
> *Discipline is the ability to say 'no' to what is sin, to say 'yes' to what is right, and to say 'I will' to what ought to be done."*[7]

 ## *From My Heart*

How many people do you know who lack *enkrateia?* Sounds like they must have some serious disorder, doesn't it? They do! It is called laziness. *Enkrateia* is the Greek word for self-control.

Self-control, or self-discipline, is almost a forgotten word in many Christian homes today. How many women do you know who faithfully discipline themselves to spend even fifteen minutes in God's Word each day? Yet a survey revealed that the average women spends thirty hours a week watching television. That is more than four hours a day! Let's assume the average Christian women watches only half that much. That is still two hours of television a day. Filling our minds with television won't do much to help us on to godliness.

I'm speaking from experience, ladies. I once was hooked on soap operas. My children were small, and it seemed I was busy all the time. I never had time to read my Bible, but I always had an hour to watch my show. I began to feel guilty because I had time for television but not for my Bible. To appease my conscience, I would hurriedly read my Bible during the commercials. However, the more I read my Bible, the less I needed my soap opera. God's Word changed my appetite and my mind.

As women who desire to live for God, we must learn to discipline our minds. Our actions are the products of our thoughts (Proverbs 23:7).

As we end our study, would you pray this prayer with me?

"Lord, help me to control my mind and my imaginations. Without any warning, they can suddenly become turbulent and unrestrained, I give them to You. Put them under Your control. Attack every area of my mind. Manage it; govern it. Think Your thoughts through me. Help me always to remember, 'I may not be what I think I am, but I am what I think.' Amen."

From Your Heart

Look back at your answer to question 20. What steps do you need to take to begin to gain self-control in this area? Are you willing to start right now?

Remember: *Love* is not a feeling but a choice. *Joy* is unaffected by people or circumstances. *Peace* is living without worry or fear. *Long-suffering* is going on with a knife in your heart. *Gentleness* is being kind, tenderhearted, and forgiving. *Goodness* is having a servant's heart. *Faithfulness* is being dependable and loyal. *Meekness* is humility that allows you to submit. *Self-control* is learning when to say no.

God bless you—and don't give up the struggle. You can learn to walk in the Spirit and enjoy all the benefits of the Spirit-controlled life.

Juanita

Notes:

1. De Jong, p. 130.

2. Elliot, *Discipline: The Glad Surrender,* pp. 103, 104.

3. Eleanor L. Doan, compiler, *The Speaker's Sourcebook* (Grand Rapids: Zondervan Publishing House, 1960), p. 221.

4. Max E. Anders, *30 Days to Understanding the Christian Life* (Brentwood, TN: Wolgemuth & Hyatt, Publishers, 1990), p. 43.

5. De Jong, p. 131.

6. *Timeless Insights* (Atlanta, GA: Walk Thru the Bible Ministries, 1991), June 1991, p. 29.

7. White, p. 74.

LEADER'S
GUIDE

SUGGESTIONS FOR LEADERS

The effectiveness of a group Bible study usually depends on two things: (1) the leader herself, and (2) the ladies' commitment to prepare beforehand and interact during the study. You cannot totally control the second factor, but you have total control over the first one. These brief suggestions will help you be an effective Bible study leader.

You will want to prepare each lesson a week in advance. During the week, read supplemental material. The books from which the quotations are taken and that are listed in the notes section of each lesson are good supplements, as are magazine articles and Bible commentaries. Look for illustrations in the everyday events of your life as well as in the lives of others.

Encourage the ladies in the Bible study to complete each lesson before the meeting itself. This will make the discussion more interesting. You can suggest that ladies answer two or three questions a day as part of their daily Bible reading time rather than trying to do the entire lesson at one sitting.

You may also want to encourage the ladies to memorize the key verse for each lesson. (This is the verse that is printed in italics at the start of each lesson.) If possible, print the verses on 3" x 5" cards to distribute each week. If you cannot do this, suggest that the ladies make their own cards and keep them in a prominent place throughout the week.

The physical setting in which you meet will have some bearing on the study itself. An informal circle of chairs, chairs around a table, someone's living room or family room—these types of settings encourage people to relax and participate. In addition to an informal setting, create an atmosphere in which ladies feel free to participate and be themselves.

During the discussion time, here are a few guidelines to observe:

• Don't do all the talking. This study is not designed to be a lecture.

• Encourage discussion on each question by adding ideas and questions.

• Don't discuss controversial issues that will divide the group. (Differences of opinion are healthy; divisions are not.)

• Don't allow one lady to dominate the discussion. Use statements such as these to draw others into the study: "Let's hear from someone on this side of the room" (the side opposite the dominant talker); "Let's hear from someone who has not shared yet today."

• Stay on the subject. The tendency toward tangents is always possible in a discussion. One of your responsibilities as the leader is to keep the group on track.

• Don't get bogged down on a question that interests only one person.

You may want to use the last fifteen minutes of the scheduled time for prayer. If you have a large group of ladies, divide into smaller groups for prayer. You could call this the "Share and Care Time."

If you have a morning Bible study, encourage the ladies to go out for lunch with someone else from time to time. This is a good way to get acquainted with new ladies. Occasionally you could plan a time when ladies bring their own lunches or salads to share and have lunch together. These activities help promote fellowship and friendship in the group.

The formats that follow are suggestions only. You can plan your own format, use one of these, or adapt one of these to your needs.

2-hour Bible Study

10:00—10:15 Coffee and fellowship time
10:15—10:30 Get-acquainted time
             Have two ladies take five minutes each to tell something about themselves and their families.
             Also use this time to make announcements and, if appropriate, take an offering for the baby-sitters.
10:30—11:45 Bible study
             Leader guides discussion of the questions in the day's lesson.
11:45—12:00 Prayer time

2-hour Bible Study

10:00—10:45 Bible lesson
             Leader teaches a lesson on the content of the material. No discussion during this time.
10:45—11:00 Coffee and fellowship
11:00—11:45 Discussion time
             Divide into small groups with an appointed leader for each group. Discuss the questions in the day's lesson.
11:45—12:00 Prayer time

1½-hour Bible Study

10:00—10:30 Bible study
             Leader guides discussion of half the questions in the day's lesson.
10:30—10:45 Coffee and fellowship
10:45—11:15 Bible study
             Leader continues discussion of the questions in the day's lesson.
11:15—11:30 Prayer time

Answers for Leader's Use

Information inside parentheses ( ) is additional instruction for the group leader.

LESSON 1

1. Dead in trespasses and sin.

2. Spiritually dead; without the power to keep from sinning. People sin because they are sinners.

3. *Ephesians 2:1*—Dead *in* sin. *Romans 6:2*—Dead *to* sin.

4. We are separated from sin's control, or authority, in our lives. Christ died not only to cancel the penalty of past sins, but also to cancel the power of present sin.

5. As long as we are in this body, sin will continue to try to control us. Daily we must put off the flesh and allow the new nature (the Holy

Spirit) to be in control. Each day we choose to yield to the control of the flesh or the Spirit.

6. We know we were baptized, or placed, into Christ's death. Positionally, His death became our death. We know we have been set free from sin's bondage through Christ's death and resurrection. Our old sin nature has been crucified with Him (Gal. 2:20).

7. An emotion is a strong feeling. I must, with strong feelings, believe the facts I know are true. Sin is no longer my master, but Christ is. Christ has set me free. I now have new life in Him.

8. I can know I don't have to sin. I can believe I don't have to sin. But these facts will be of no value to me unless I choose, by an act of my will, not to sin by yielding the members of my body to do right.

9. We cause ourselves to sin. We do not have to sin; we choose to sin.

10. Christ now lives in us.

11. By the indwelling Holy Spirit.

12. The life of Christ dwells in the born-again believer.

13. Before salvation, we had only the old nature. After salvation, we still have the flesh urging us to do wrong and the new nature urging us to do right.

14. (a) Sexual. (b) Religious. (c) Domestic or personal relationships. (d) Social.

15. Crucify the flesh.

16. By obedience to the truths of God's Word. I choose to become a servant of righteousness. In other words, I choose to obey the truths of God's Word.

17. Sacrifice always involves giving. I must give up my rights, my desires, my will.

18. (Ask the ladies to consider prayerfully what God wants them to do.)

19. When we are walking in the Spirit, we will know and others will know by the outward evidences of love, patience, kindness, etc.

LESSON 2

1. Self-love—love of self; conceit; selfishness. Self-esteem—(1) belief in one's self; self-respect; (2) undue pride in one's self; conceit. These two definitions of self-esteem seem to contradict one another. I think the first definition is a picture of a healthy self-image, the second a picture of an unhealthy self-image, full of pride and self-centeredness.

2. You will not find any verses. Some people want to use Matthew 22:39 ("Thou shalt love thy neighbour as thyself") as support for self-love. However, the verse does not say to love one's self, but to love one's neighbor the same way one loves herself.

3. We are to esteem others better than ourselves. We are to hate our own life. The Greek word for "hate" means "to love less." We are to love ourselves less than we love Christ and others.

4. God never tells us to love ourselves. Matthew 22:39 presupposes that we already do. We love ourselves because of the self-centered, sinful nature with which we were born.

5. This person is overly consumed with self. She feels sorry for

herself because others aren't providing the love, approval, and protection she wants from them. Self-pity thinks of what it can take in, not what it can give out. Suicide is produced by thinking too much about self, saying, "I don't have to take this; I can't take this any longer; poor me; nobody loves me."

6. We get too consumed with self, which leads to this kind of thinking: "I deserve a better life; I must learn to get in touch with myself; I must learn to assert myself; I have to look out for number one." Life centers around me, myself, and I.

7. Rejection by parents, abusive relationships, lack of money and education, lack of love and understanding from others.

8. Jesus Christ is the only One Who can meet all of our needs. Because mankind is sinful, people will always fail to meet all our expectations. Many people have felt very secure in a relationship only to have it end in rejection and heartache. Material things only give us a false sense of significance and security. Jesus Christ is the only One Who will never fail us.

9. *Jeremiah 31:3*—God loves us unconditionally. *1 John 1:9*—We can be forgiven. *Psalm 139:1–4*—God fully knows us and fully accepts us.

10. *Matthew 25:21*—Christ will give us His approval for a life of obedience to Him. *Hebrews 13:5*—Jesus Christ will never leave us or forsake us. *Matthew 25:35–40*—Christ appreciates even the smallest things we do for Him.

11. *Agape* love gives out to others regardless of whether my needs are being met. It is self-less, others-centered. Self-love cares about self first.

12. When we are born-again, we become new creations; all the past is forgiven; we have a new lease on life. We now have Christ's power to help and strengthen us for every situation and person we will ever face. However, learning to avail ourselves of this power and putting it into practice in our lives is a daily process. It is part of the sanctification process described in lesson 1.

13. Paul was mistreated, abused, and dishonored. (When we have been mistreated, it is easy to develop a spirit of self-pity. When this happens, we may be too wrapped up in our problems to see the friends who could help us. Notice Paul's remembrance of his friends when he was in prison; Colossians 4:7–14.)

14. Paul was strengthened by the power of God to face every situation in life.

15. *1 Corinthians 3:10*—He was a wise master builder. *1 Corinthians 4:1*—He was a steward of the mysteries of God. *1 Corinthians 4:15, 16*—He ranked himself higher than ten thousand tutors. *1 Corinthians 15:10*—He realized he had "laboured more abundantly than they all" because of the grace of God "which was with me."

16. She is letting fleshly, sinful emotions control her.

17. *Psalm 51:1, 2, 12*—Acknowledge sin and accept God's forgiveness, cleansing, and restoration. *2 Peter 1:2–4*—Daily fill her mind with the "knowledge of God, and of Jesus, our Lord." Christ will give her, through His divine power, everything she needs to live a godly life. *Galatians 5:16, 22, 23*—Choose to be controlled by the Holy Spirit.

18. Jesus sets forth self-denial, not self-love, as the way to enter into a proper relationship with God and others.

19. Saying no to our selfish, fleshly desires each day.

20. I must realize that in my flesh dwells the potential for me to become a criminal. I must put this mean, sinful, selfish flesh to death daily, or I will find myself fulfilling the lusts of the flesh listed in Galatians 5:19–21.

21. We must daily present ourselves to God as a living sacrifice. Sacrifice means giving up something. I must daily live a palms-up life. I must open my hands and turn loose of everything I hold tightly. I must say to God, "Give what You want, and take what You want; I turn loose completely."

22. *John 1:12*—As His sons (children). *1 Corinthians 3:16*—As His temple and indwelt by His Spirit. *Romans 5:10*—As reconciled to Him. *Romans 5:1*—As justified (made right with God). *2 Corinthians 5:20*—As His ambassadors, or representatives. *2 Corinthians 5:21*—As having His righteousness. *Jeremiah 31:3*—As loved unconditionally.

LESSON 3

1. In born-again believers, those who have received Christ as their Savior.

2. At the exact moment a person receives Christ as Savior.

3. Born-again believers, those who have new life in Christ.

4. "Be filled with the Spirit."

5. To be Christ-centered is to desire to know Christ better each day and to be more like Him.

6. So we will obey and do God's Word, not merely hear it.

7. A spirit of surrender and sacrifice; surrendering my will to God's will.

8. (a) No; God will never make us obey Him. (b) We will want to obey because we have a yielded spirit that wants God's will in our lives.

9. It is a continual filling, a daily process, not a once-for-all act.

10. By a deliberate and willful choice to say no to sin and yes to God.

11. We will want to sing with God's people and be with them.

12. (a) No; this verse does not necessarily mean outward singing. (b) We can have a song in our heart in spite of circumstances.

13. We can be grateful God is in control and knows what is going on, even when we don't understand.

14. When we have the right view of God, we will not find it difficult to submit to fellow believers.

15. *Love*—A spirit that thinks of others more than self. *Joy*—A song in the heart that is not dependent on people or circumstances but comes from our relationship with Christ. *Peace*—A confident assurance that nothing touches my life without God's permission. *Long-suffering*—Patient endurance that does not retaliate or run away from difficult circumstances or people. *Gentleness*—A kind, sweet spirit toward others. *Goodness*—Kindness that is demonstrated in doing kind and thoughtful things for others. *Faithfulness*—The ability to be trusted and depended on in our relationships. *Meekness*—Strength that allows us to have a humble, submissive spirit. *Self-control*—The ability to control the desires of the flesh or to motivate the flesh.

LESSON 4

1. His love is an everlasting love.

2. (a) Very few people understand unconditional love, and even fewer people demonstrate it. (b) (Ask the ladies to examine their hearts in this regard.) (c) (Ask the ladies to share recent incidents when God gave them the grace to practice unconditional love.)

3. Giving of Himself for others. When we picture our love compared to God's love, it looks something like this:

AGAPE LOVE—God's kind of love; selfless: What can I do for you?

A-GIVE-ME LOVE—Our kind of love; selfish: What can I get for me?

4. As Christ loved us. This kind of love is demonstrated in selfless giving, expecting nothing in return.

5. (a) No; God never asks us to do anything He will not empower us to do. (b) Denying self and living a Christlike life.

6. We must exchange our strength for Christ's strength. We do this by daily drawing close to Christ, reading His Word, and gaining new strength from the Word.

7. Christ has commanded us to love the unlovely. If we want to be obedient Christians, we must respond to Christ's commands in a positive way.

8. The root of envy is selfishness. I want what you have, or you can't have what I have. I must forget self and esteem others better than myself. When I think as Christ thinks, my thoughts will be, "How can I serve you?"

9. Love is not big-headed but big-hearted. Love wants honor for Christ and for others, not for self.

10. Our own families, the ones we love the most. We would never treat a guest the way we often treat family members.

11. Could it be that we are too selfish? A self-centered person says, "I don't have time to listen to your problems; I have enough of my own to handle."

12. (a) Our temperament or our parents. (b) Our selfish nature that wants its own way.

13. (a) Get your mind on Christ and off people or circumstances that are bothering you. (b) God's Word. Write out a list of verses, and carry them around with you until you have them memorized. If you have the book *Trials—Don't Resent Them as Intruders,* use the "Why Sink When You Can Swim" verses on pages 49 and 50.

14. We must forget how we feel and choose to do right whether we feel like it or not. If we know God commands but choose to disobey them, we are sinning.

15. It may cost us a relationship we hold dear, but we must decide who is first in our lives: Christ or others.

16. When we realize God can use these trials to help us grow spiritually, we will be more likely to endure them and not run from them or resent them as intrusions in our lives.

17. Love looks beyond a person's faults and sees a person with great needs. Those needs cause us to say, "What is this person's problem? How can I help him?"

18. Never give up on a person. God can save and change the worst of sinners.

19. Christ did not retaliate or take vengeance into His own hands.

20. Everlasting, unconditional love.

LESSON 5

1. Rejoice (be joyful) always.

2. When a believer abides in Christ's presence, He is a continual source of joy and strength in her life. When a branch is pulled away from the vine, the sap, the source of strength, can no longer flow into it. The same is true in her life. If she does not stay closely connected to the Vine, the Lord Jesus, she loses her source of strength and joy.

3. *Psalm 34:8*—God is always good, even when we don't understand His goodness. We must always remember that a loving Father always has His child's best interest at heart. *Psalm 145:17*—God is righteous and holy, and all He does is right. Something may not make sense from our perspective, but it is right from His perspective. *Jeremiah 31:3*—God's love is an everlasting, unconditional love. He loves us regardless of our actions. *Hebrews 13:5 and 6*—God is always with us to help us and sustain us.

4. (a) Happiness comes from a root word meaning "chance." Having all your circumstances fall into place just right might result in happiness. Joy results from walking in close relationship with Jesus Christ. Joy can be present even during your most difficult trials. Happiness depends on happenings; joy depends on your relationship with Jesus Christ. (b) I heard this explanation: Joy is the smile of the soul, and peace is serenity of the soul.

5. A surrendered life; sacrificing our will for God's will.

6. I loosen my grip on every person and thing in my life and say, "Lord, it all belongs to You. Give what You want; take what You want. I give it all to You."

7. We get our eyes on the circumstances and people who are causing the stress, and we take our eyes off the Lord and His promises. If joy is absent in our lives, we need to check how much time we are spending in God's presence. How many of His promises are we claiming?

8. By willingly sinning against God.

9. When we are out of fellowship with Christ and have unconfessed sin in our lives, we are filled with turmoil, guilt, and fear instead of love, joy, and peace. The situation is similar to that of a child who has disobeyed his parents and knows he is going to be punished.

10. We must confess our sin and accept God's forgiveness. Then our relationship with Christ and our joy are restored. (Also see James 4:8–10.)

11. (Have the ladies share some of their experiences and how they are dealing with them.)

12. *Nehemiah 8:10*—The joy of the Lord is your strength. The joyous relationship you have with Christ gives strength beyond yourself. *2 Corinthians 12:9 and 10*—When you are weak, Christ gives you His strength, and this strength is a cause for joy. You do not have to let circumstances or people control you.

13. Marital problems; rebellious children; family conflicts (such as in-laws); financial problems; job insecurity; poor health; death in the family; church problems.

14. Good health; peace in the home and family; answered prayers; encouragement from fellow believers; God's Word; financial security.

15. Keep your mind stayed on Christ by meditating on and memorizing God's Word. Replace negative thoughts (your problems) with positive things (God's Word).

16. *Philippians 3:13 and 14*—Quit saying, "If only," and forget the past. Quit saying, "What if," and forget about the future. Keep your eyes focused on Christ. *Philippians 4:6 and 7*—Stop worrying, start praying, keep thanking, and enjoy the peace of God.

17. In every circumstance God allows in our lives, good or bad, we are to be thankful.

18. It is a matter of the soul. It is a fixed confidence in God that keeps our troubles from immobilizing us. It is not self-centered, saying, "Woe is me." We may not always have a smile on our faces, but there is a smile in our soul and a peace that says, "All is well; God is in control."

19. (Ask the ladies to tell of people whom they know who are experiencing the joy of the Lord in their lives.)

20. Personal answers.

LESSON 6

1. A restless, troubled person without peace.

2. A person has peace with God when she accepts by faith what Jesus Christ did on Calvary for her: shed His blood to take away her sin.

3. (Ask the ladies to prayerfully examine their relationship with Jesus Christ. Give a further explanation of salvation as the Spirit leads you.)

4. Christ Jesus.

5. An inner resource of strength that allows us to overcome anxiety and turmoil in our lives. It is a strength that surpasses our understanding. It is described in Philippians 4:7.

6. We can have this peace in every situation of life. The key word is "keep." The Hebrew word means "maintain," or "preserve."

7. I use my "Why Sink When You Can Swim" verses. (See *Trials—Don't Resent Them as Intruders,* pages 49 and 50.) Take out the "sinking thinking" and put in "gazing and praising": gazing on God's Word and praising God for His promises.

8. We must *allow* God's peace to rule in our hearts. Again, it is a choice, an act of the will.

9. (Have some ladies share their answers.)

10. (Again, ask the ladies to share a few up-to-date experiences.)

11. (a) Everyone battles the four P's: people, problems, perplexities, and possibilities. List various situations that fall under these four categories. (b) A survey cited these common fears: fear of being rejected, fear of losing control, fear of being inadequate, fear of sickness and death, fear of the future.

12. "I don't believe You can take care of me."

13. God is concerned about even the smallest details of our lives.

Every time a sparrow falls, He sees it; every time a hair falls from your head, God sees it and changes the count.

14. We don't really believe that God cares, or we don't really feel He can take care of our situation.

15. (a) Worry. (b) Pray about everything. (c) Thank the Lord for everything. (d) Peace that passes all understanding.

16. (a) A command. (b) God wants us to live peaceably with others.

17. (a) Personal answers. (b) God does not want our sacrifices until we have been reconciled to our brother. Go to the person and try to resolve the problem.

18. When we put ourselves first, we are not esteeming others better than ourselves. Caring for others first will solve the problems in most relationships.

19. (Have the ladies share their thoughts.)

LESSON 7

1. Long-suffering is from two Greek words meaning "long temper." Long-suffering is the opposite of short-tempered. Someone has given it this definition: "Self-restraint that does not hastily retaliate a wrong, bears pain and trials without complaint, despite opposition, difficulty, or adversity."

2. (a) Personal answers. (b) (Ask the ladies to do some honest evaluating.)

3. One of the characteristics of *agape* love is that it "endureth all things," which is a picture of patience. Joy and peace allow us to endure with the joy of the Lord in our lives and serenity in our souls.

4. Trials develop enduring patience. The Chinese people have a word picture for perseverance, or patience: continuing on with a knife in your heart.

5. (a) Job. (b) Patience.

6. We have so many questions: Why this? Why now? Why me? What next?

7. *Job 1:21*—The Lord does good (He gives), and He also sends troubles (He takes away). *Job 2:10*—Shouldn't we accept trouble as well as good from God?

8. After seven days of thinking of his calamity (Job 2:13), Job began to experience depression and despair. His heart and mind were filled with anguish and turmoil.

9. "Tell me what charges You have against me"; in other words, "What have I done to deserve this?"

10. We often think surely God has forgotten us; does He really know how we feel? Feeling forsaken is part of the process of becoming like Christ. Christ was forsaken on the cross when He said, "My God, my God why have you forsaken me?" Job's greatest loss was not his family and possessions but his loss of the sense of God's presence with him.

11. Personal answers.

12. (a) No. (b) "Will you try to correct Me?"

13. God is beyond understanding. God wanted to teach Job to love and trust Him, not because of what He did or didn't give him, but just because of Who He is—a sovereign God.

14. Personal answers.

15. Examples of situations that call for great patience are a handicapped child, an unsaved husband, a workaholic husband, a rebellious child, difficulties with a roommate, an unsatisfactory job situation, physical handicap or illness, financial problems.

16. When you begin to think of what others are enduring, your trials may not seem so unbearable.

17. When we leave their judgment with God instead of giving them our judgment, they receive blessing from us instead of cursing.

18. While we are being patient, God can take the deliberately harmful acts of others and turn them into good for us and others.

19. Practice *agape* love. *Agape* love covers a multitude of sins; it looks beyond a person's faults and sees his or her need for our long-suffering.

20. Use the situation as an opportunity to forgive another as Christ has forgiven us.

21. We begin to manipulate and scheme to try to get things done. I have this note on my refrigerator to remind me not to do this: "Dear Juanita, I don't need your help today! Love, God."

22. (a) Personal answers. (b) Personal answers. (c) (Encourage the ladies to be specific.) God has told us to be kind, patient, and forgiving toward others, but He never told us we should expect to be treated that way by others. We lose patience with people many times because of misplaced expectations. God is the only One Who will always be fair, Who is always kind, loving, and forgiving.

LESSON 8

1. Gentleness is mildness in dealing with others; it is careful not to be insensitive to the rights of others.

2. (Ask the ladies for their thoughts. Also suggest the woman described in Proverbs 31: "She stretcheth out her hand to the poor; yea, she reacheth forth her hands to the needy" [v. 20]; "In her tongue is the law of kindness" [v. 26].)

3. Mercy is compassion or forbearance shown especially to an offender. You cannot be genuinely kind without being merciful, and it is impossible to be merciful without being kind. Genuine care and concern will offer compassion to those who don't deserve it.

4. We will treat others the way we would like to be treated. We will be sensitive to the suffering and sorrow of others and look for ways to relieve that suffering.

5. Being tenderhearted and forgiving.

6. They are kind to those who are kind to them and courteous to those who reciprocate.

7. We will take abuse without retaliation. We will even be able to love the unlovely and those who hate us.

8. 70 x 7 = 490. This is such a large number that we will not be able to keep record of the offenses. In other words, keep forgiving as long as forgiveness is needed.

9. A servant's spirit. This spirit is of divine origin and belongs to those who are controlled by the Holy Spirit.

10. God will return love and kindness to us in ways we never thought

of. Deeds of kindness shown to others in compassion and mercy will not go unrewarded.

11. Christ counts our kindness to others as kindness to Himself.

12. Possible answers include making personal visits or phone calls to the sick and lonely; writing notes of encouragement to people passing through deep waters and fiery trials; taking a meal to a family with illness. (Ask the ladies to share other ideas.)

13. Christ was meek and lowly. He was never stressed out or in a frenzy. Christ was always a picture of perfect peace and rest.

14. They will feel at rest around us because of our restful, Christlike spirit.

15. (Ask the ladies to take time to evaluate themselves and give specific answers. They do not have to share their answers.)

16. (Ask the ladies to consider following the suggestions.)

17. A nursing mother shares her own life with her child. She takes time with the child and spends much energy caring for him. She also has patience with him, realizing he is only a child. A mother's love suffers long, is kind, and protects the child.

18. We must be willing to share our time and energies with other people and be patient and long-suffering with them.

LESSON 9

1. (a) (Have a few ladies share their answers.) (b) Goodness is kindness in action—a helping hand as well as a caring heart.

2. He went about doing good.

3. To do good works.

4. Walking is a daily thing we do without thinking about it. In a similar way, doing good deeds should come automatically; we should do them without even giving a thought.

5. Raising children, lodging strangers, washing saints' feet, relieving the afflicted.

6. Housewives often feel tied down and unfulfilled because they don't get dressed up to go somewhere each day. They regard cleaning house, changing diapers, and cooking meals as unimportant jobs that anybody could do. But these "mundane" jobs can be viewed as good works.

7. Personal answers.

8. Personal answers.

9. Our husbands, children, and parents.

10. "All men" includes unbelievers. It may be that hateful neighbor next door or the unruly children across the street.

11. You always do good and help the needy.

12. A do-gooder or a goody-goody.

13. Additional answers include writing a note or sending a card of encouragement; taking someone out for lunch; having someone in your home for a meal; driving a person to an appointment; baby-sitting; sitting with someone in the hospital; getting groceries for an elderly person or shut-in.

14. God's gracious provision in making us sufficient for every job He gives us to do.

15. *Eyes*—We see what needs to be done and go about meeting those needs without being asked. *Ears*—We listen to the cries of the broken-hearted and the pleas of the needy. They don't want our advice as much as they want a listening ear. *Hands*—We reach out a hand to those sinking in despair and hopelessness. We give the hurting ones a hug that says, "I care." *Feet*—We walk out of our way to do whatever we can, whenever we can. *Strong back*—We are to bear one another's burdens (Gal. 6:2).

16. (a) Personal answers. (b) Esteem others better than ourselves.

17. To be an example of how we are to serve others.

18. (Have the ladies share their feelings on this subject.)

19. One day that person will hear Him say, "Well done, good and faithful servant."

LESSON 10

1. God is the only One Who is always faithful and will never fail.

2. When we read God's Word and our history books, we see God's faithfulness to all generations, right down to our present, ungodly generation. This earth may be polluted and deteriorating, but it will stand the tests of time until God destroys it and makes the new heaven and the new earth (2 Pet. 3:10–13; Rev. 21:1).

3. He will keep His promises and show mercy to those who love Him.

4. He hears our prayers, and, because He is faithful, He will answer.

5. He is our example of a faithful servant.

6. (a) Yes. (b) Isaiah 50:7—When Christ was brought before Pilate, men beat Him and plucked out His beard, but He would not be turned aside by the suffering and shame. How could He keep His commitment of love to a lost world? "For the LORD God will help me." Matthew 26:51–56—Jesus could have had twelve legions of angels (72,000; a legion was 6,000) who would have come at the Father's bidding, but He knew it was not the Father's will for Him to be rescued.

7. "It is finished" indicates Christ completed the task He had come to do: make possible our salvation.

8. If we want to be Christlike and follow in His footsteps, we will be faithful. We will commit ourselves to our responsibilities and vows and finish the tasks God has given us to do. We will be faithful when it is easy and when it is hard, when we feel like it and when we don't feel like it.

9. (Have the ladies think carefully about this question. Loss of interest and no sense of commitment can cause unfaithfulness.)

10. Negligent, unfaithful, careless.

11. (Be sure the ladies have taken time to circle one of the answers.)

12. (Ask some ladies to read their answers to the class.)

13. *Proverbs 28:20*—A faithful person will abound with blessings. *Matthew 25:21*—She will hear Christ say, "Well done, good and faithful servant."

14. Christ, our mates, our relatives, our friends and neighbors, our employers, our country.

15. *Hebrews 10:25*—She attends worship services with other believers. *Psalm 100:2*—She serves the Lord gladly wherever and whenever she can. *Psalm 119:16*—She spends time in God's Word.

16. (a) (Have a few ladies read their answers.) (b) She will stick with you through thick and thin.

17. A loyal friend cares enough about you to point out your shortcomings.

18. Why am I doing this: to help or to hurt? Am I doing this only to make me look good and my friend look bad? Do I really love this person?

19. The attitude that says, "I deserve to be happy; I don't have to take this" overrides the commitment the partners made to God and to each other.

20. Christ said His disciples would suffer persecution. When persecution comes, we should not run from it, but endure it for Christ's sake because we want to obey Him.

21. Holy.

LESSON 11

1. (Ask ladies to share their illustrations. I like the illustration of a meek horse. A horse is meek when it can be neck-reined, which means it easily submits to the will of the master. He does not have to yank and pull to get the horse to go where he wants. He just gently lays the reins to one side or the other of the neck to indicate which way the horse should go. A meek person easily submits to the will of another.)

2. It takes great power to be meek, to submit to the will of another.

3. Christ said, "Not my will, but thine, be done." In the crises of life as well as daily decisions, we need to say the same thing.

4. Since God's way is perfect and our will is His will, we will not resent what comes into our lives. We will recognize that any circumstance has to have His stamp of approval before it touches us.

5. The palms-up life says, "Thy will be done" and means it. We turn loose of everything we are hanging on to and open ourselves to whatever God wants to give. We put our palms up and say, "Give what You want, and take what You want."

6. We will realize and acknowledge that all we have and all we are have come from the hand of God.

7. The spirit of humility helps us know we do not know it all and opens our hearts to the truth.

8. A proud person thinks she is better than others; therefore, she has difficulty submitting to others.

9. A spirit of servitude.

10. Ministering to the needs of others as exemplified by the Lord Jesus.

11. We need to realize that we can be tempted to sin as well. In addition, it is easy to be overbearing when we are right and the other person is wrong. We need to remember that we want to restore the person, not destroy her.

12. If we deal with a person who opposes us in arrogance, we may win the argument but lose the person in the process. We want the person to see the error of her way, not just our way.

13. We must esteem others better than ourselves.

14. (Ask volunteers to share their answers.)

15. They don't obey verses 18–21. When we are controlled by the

Holy Spirit, we will be willing to submit to others.

16. The husband is the head or manager of the home, and the wife is to follow his leadership.

17. A supporter and responder to her mate; a help to him.

18. (a) The Father. (b) The Father. (c) The husband. (d) The husband.

19. Christ knew exactly Who He was and why He had come to earth.

20. (a) No. (b) He humbled Himself and was obedient.

21. If we want to be Christlike, we must have a serving, submissive, humble spirit.

LESSON 12

1. Self-control is the inner strength that enables us to please God by saying no when we should say no and yes when we should say yes.

2. A good thing, such as food, can have power over us instead of our having power over it if we do not exercise self-control.

3. Like a city with broken-down walls. A city without walls was vulnerable to the attacks of the enemy. Likewise, an undisciplined person, one who lacks self-control, is vulnerable to all kinds of trouble and is open prey for her enemy, Satan.

4. Possible answers include overeating, drinking, impure sexual desires, laziness.

5. Prayer (and Bible study as well).

6. Two common excuses are not enough time and the inability to be alone. (Have the ladies share some difficulties they face in this vital area of their lives.)

7. (a) Television. (b) We must learn to control it, or it will control us. If we can't learn to control the television, then we need to get rid of it.

8. Personal answers.

9. (Have volunteers suggest some solutions.)

10. Whatever is planted in the mind—whether pure or impure—will grow. These thoughts will turn into actions unless something is done to stifle the growth.

11. The verse describes the kind of thoughts we should have: true, honest, just, pure, lovely, of good report.

12. Lay aside all sins and weights that slow us down, and look to Jesus.

13. (Encourage the ladies to write specific areas of struggle. Answers do not need to be shared aloud.)

14. We must daily exchange our will for God's will so we can say yes to God and no to sin. For some ladies, this involves stopping some things they are doing. For others, it means starting some positive actions in their lives.

15. (Encourage the ladies to be honest in their self-evaluation.)

16. (Read the six questions with the ladies. Encourage honest evaluation.)

17. We must choose to walk in the Spirit rather than gratify fleshly lusts. We must recognize the battle that goes on between the flesh and the Spirit and choose to feed the new nature ("delight in the law of God").

18. The desire to please the flesh is stronger than the desire to please God.

19. (Some ladies may want to share what things were like in their homes before they began to exercise self-control.)

20. (Encourage the ladies to be specific. Total honesty with one's self and God is one of the first steps in conquering self and exercising control in one's life.)